Triumph of Spirit
Book One

Healing and Activating with the
Triumph of Spirit Archetypes

I0109036

Version 1.11

To purchase TOSAS cards and books,
https://tosas.lightningpath.org/purchase/

As above in consciousness,
so below in matter

The Triumph of Spirit
Book One

Healing and Activating with the
Triumph of Spirit Archetypes

Mike Sosteric

Lightning Path Press

St Albert, Alberta, Canada

press.lightningpath.org

Library of Congress Cataloging-in-Publication Data
Sosteric, Michael, 1963-, author,
The book of triumph: healing and activating with the Triumph of Spirit System / Dr. Michael Sosteric.

ISBN 978-1-897455-62-3 (bound)
ISBN 978-1-897455-61-6 (booklet and cards)

1. Tarot. 2. Archetype (Psychology). 3. Spiritual healing-Miscellanea. 4. Mental healing-Miscellanea. I. Title.

BF1879.T2S544 2013 133.3'2424 C2013-904878-2

Table of Contents

PREFACE

The book that you have in your hand now, the *Triumph of Spirit Book One: Healing and Activating with the Triumph of Spirit*, is one of a series of books devoted to the dissemination of a **New Energy Archetype System**[1] entitled the *Triumph of Spirit Archetype System*, or just TOSAS for short.

The TOSAS (pronounced TOE-SIS) is a collection of **new energy** archetypes presented in text and image form. TOSAS "scripture" is contained in four books, one booklet (included with the boxed card

---

[1] Archetypes are ideas (either unconscious or conscious) that provide you with answers to a **big question**, like "Who am I?" or "Why am I here?" For example, if you ask the question, "What is my purpose for incarnating on this planet?" and if you answer the question, "So I can learn my lessons and grow as a spiritual soul," this answer is an archetype because it answers your big question.

New Energy archetypes are archetypes that encourage (individual and collective) awakening, (full) activation (of the body's energy systems), and ascension/connection to higher Consciousness.

A "system" is a collection of interacting, interrelated, or interdependent elements that together form a complex whole.

set), and an accompanying archetype deck, the **Triumph of Spirit Archetype Deck.** The Triumph of Spirit deck consists of twenty-two beautifully rendered archetype cards, each of which conveys a single, but highly interrelated, new energy archetype.

Each of the four TOSAS books explores the new energy archetypes from a different angle, and to different depths. The book you have in your hand explores the archetypes primarily in a healing and **activation**[2] (i.e., empowerment) context. Towards the goal of encouraging healing and activation, this book provides synoptic overviews of each of the twenty-two TOSAS archetype cards, as well as spiritual, assessment, and therapeutic meanings for each.

Because this book focuses on emotional, psychological, spiritual, and physical healing, leading towards awakening, activation, and ascension, the TOSAS system and deck are superlative additions to any therapeutic or healing toolkit.

---

[2] Activation (a.k.a. "empowerment") occurs when an individual embraces creative power and becomes an active and empowered change agent in the world. See https://spiritwiki.lightningpath.org/Activation.

The TOSAS will be of interest to healers, professionals, therapists, and students of the **Lightning Path** (LP)[3] where it provides extended, intermediate-level activation training and guidance, with a particular focus on reprogramming negative thinking patterns and the establishment of pure and consistent **Right Thought.**[4] As LP students will know, right thought is thought that moves us towards spiritual connection,[5] while **Wrong Thought** is thought that damages the body and mind and discourages/distorts that same connection. The TOSAS is evolving. For a list of books devoted to the study of new energy archetypes and right thought, see https://www.lightningpath.org/activate/.

---

[3] The Lightning Path (LP) is a sophisticated, modern, and authentic system of human development that helps you heal, awaken, activate, and ascend (i.e. connect) to a higher level of Consciousness. For information, see https://www.lightningpath.org/lp-nutshell.

[4] https://spiritwiki.lightningpath.org/Right_Thought.

[5] Connection is the LP term for what occurs when your body connects to its own higher Consciousness. For more see https://spiritwiki.lightningpath.org/Connection.

WHAT IS THE TOSAS?

Greetings and welcome to the *Triumph of Spirit Archetype System (TOSAS)*. The TOSAS is a collection of archetypes, organized and presented via a set of books and archetype cards. For your information, **archetypes**[6] are big ideas and concepts that

1. Provide answers to **Big Questions**,[7]
2. Organize how we see and think about the world,
3. Guide and sometimes determine our actions and reactions.

Initially the idea that there is a system of ideas and archetypes that can provide us with answers, organize how we see the world, and determine our actions, and that these archetypes can be organized into a system like the TOSAS, might sound a little crazy, even scary. Nevertheless, it is a fact. From the moment we are born, we are trained (socialized) without our permission and consent into a particular

---

[6] For more on archetypes, see the SpiritWiki page at https://spiritwiki.lightningpath.org/Archetypes.

[7] Big questions are questions like "Who am I?", "Why am I here," or "What is my purpose?" See https://spiritwiki.lightningpath.org/Big_Questions.

system of archetypes. I will call the archetype system we are socialized into as children the **old energy archetype system.** This old energy system provides a collection of archetypes that answers our questions, organizes how we see the world, and shapes/determines how we act in the world.

You can see the truth of the above statement by considering one of the archetypes in the old energy system, the archetype of good versus evil. The archetype of good versus evil is something our primary and secondary agents of socialization (i.e. our parents, teachers, Churches, and certain Hollywood studios) teach us. The teaching is basic and simple. There is good and there is evil, and the two are in a constant, never-ending battle. This good versus evil archetype is pervasive and ubiquitous. Indeed, so pervasive that most people on this planet believe in the archetype of good and evil.

As noted, archetypes provide answers to big questions, organize our thinking and perception, and direct our behavior. As for **providing answers**, the good/evil archetype provides answers to the questions like, "Why do bad things happen to good people?" When people believe in the existence of good and evil, when they see things happen in the world, they use the good/evil binary to understand

and explain what is happening around them. If a bomb goes off in a crowded airport, it is not because political oppression has led to violent action on the part of an oppressed people (a more historically/sociologically informed answer), it is because an evil terrorist has set the bomb off in an attempt to undermine the good democratic citizens of the world. If one country, let us call it Politzania,[8] invades another, it is not because the invading country is imperialist and raiding the other to control their resources, it is because the good citizens of Politzania are fighting/crusading the evil, terrorist, hordes.

As for **organizing how we see and think**, the archetype of good versus evil clearly shapes how we see each other, especially those we do not like, or those who harm us in some way. When those people who have absorbed the good versus evil binary look at people who do them harm, they see it as an issue of good versus evil. This is most obvious in the case of people like Hitler, whom most people would agree is an evil person, but it also works for our neighbor next door. When somebody

---

[8] The word "Politzania" is the name of an imaginary world that destroys itself. Klaatu tells the story of Politzania on their 1977 album, *Hope.*

13

does something bad, especially when somebody harms us, those who accept this binary archetype see "them" in black versus white, good versus evil terms. Those who accept this archetype see "us" as good and "them" as evil. It does not matter what side of the proverbial divide you are on. When you accept the good/evil binary, you see the other side as evil and wrong.

In addition to providing answers to big questions and organizing our thinking, **archetypes also affect our actions**. That archetypes affect our actions is easy to see. Using the same archetype of good versus evil, if you see someone in front of you whom you judge to be acting in an evil fashion, you will feel justified, perhaps even compelled, to harm them (i.e. punish them) in some way. Notably, you will not see your actions as harm. You will see your actions as justifiable punishment. That is because an additional archetype in the old energy system is the archetype of **judgment**. According to the judgment archetype, people who are evil and do bad things deserve punishment. Punishments may vary from emotional and psychological violence through physical incarceration, execution, karmic retribution, and even eternal damnation in the fires of hell. The point is not the severity of the punishment. The point is that according to the pervasive good versus evil and judgment archetypes, if you are evil and bad, you deserve to be punished. Those who see you doing bad things will feel justified, even compelled, to punish. In this way, archetypes affect our actions.

The Western TAROT

Now you know that an archetype system is a collection of ideas and archetypes designed to

1. Provide answers to big questions,
2. Organize how we see and think about the world,
3. guide/determine our actions and reactions

You also know that as children we are all socialized into what I call an old energy archetype system. This old energy system, which I won't discuss in much detail here, but which you can learn more about in my book, *The Triumph of Spirit Book Two: Old and New Energy Archetypes,* consists of many archetypes, two of which, the "good versus evil" and "judgment" archetypes, I have already mentioned.

At this point, a reasonable question to ask might be, "Where do the old energy archetypes come from?" That is a complicated to answer. Part of the answer to that question is cultural. Old energy archetypes come in our children's fairy tales, our sacred scriptures, our myths, our legends, our comic books, and all the things that our parents teach us about the meaning of life. Archetypes come from other places as well. One of the most interesting sources of old energy archetypes, for our purposes at least, is the Western tarot system.

Many of you reading these words will have experience with the Western Tarot system. As you may know, the Western tarot is a collection of seventy-eight picture cards. The seventy-eight tarot cards are divided into two types of cards, major cards (a.k.a. major arcana) and minor cards (a.k.a. minor arcana). What you probably do not know about tarot, even if you are familiar with it, is that the twenty-two major arcana represent twenty-two of the main old energy archetypes we all learn when we are children. In other words, tarot cards are archetype cards, and the tarot deck is an **archetype deck**,[9] or archetype system. When you study a tarot deck, you are studying and old energy archetype system.

---

[9] An archetype deck is a collection of archetypes presented as images, and organized into a deck of cards. The Tarot and the TOSAS are both archetype decks. https://spiritwiki.lightningpath.org/Archetype_Deck.

If you have ever used a Western tarot deck, you will know this is true after only a little consideration. The tarot deck contains obvious old energy archetypes. For example, it contains a devil card (good/evil archetype) and a judgment card, two old energy archetypes we have already reviewed. The Western tarot, specifically the Rider-Waite tarot, [10] contains other old energy archetypes as well. Consider, for example, the Fool card. The Fool card is clearly an archetype because it answers a big question, organizes our thinking, and guides our behavior. If you ask the question "Who am I?", the Fool's answer is you are a spirit/soul in search of experience, a "fool in school," here to learn your lessons so that you can grow, evolve, and otherwise advance on some evolutionary or spiritual journey. According to the fool in school archetype, you are a student of some sort and you are here on this planet to learn lessons, prove your worth, or something like that.

---

[10] From Arthur Edward Waite, *The Pictorial Key to the Tarot: Being Fragments of a Secret Tradition under the Veil of Divination*(London: Rider, 1911). A web version of this book is available at *The Pictorial Key to the Tarot*(Sacred-texts.com, 1911).

The Rider-Waite Fool card provides a visual representation of the fool in school archetype. The individual in the card is typically described as a spiritual neophyte stepping off a cliff into incarnation to learn, advance, and grow. The dog is variously said to be the fool's "animal nature" which he must tame as part of the spiritual journey, or a guardian who will "push him to learn the lessons the Fool came here to learn."[11]

THE FOOL.

If you accept the fool in school archetype, you will see your life as a series of lessons, and you will act and respond accordingly. The powerful impact of the fool archetype is most obvious when you consider your reactions to tragedies in life. Somebody who accepts the fool archetype sees and reacts to accidents and tragedy as if they are some

_____

[11] Biddy Tarot, "Fool Tarot Card Meanings and Description," Biddy Tarot.Com, https://www.biddytarot.com/tarot-card-meanings/major-arcana/fool/.

kind of cosmic/evolutionary lesson that usually only God can understand. If you accept the fool in school archetype, when something bad happens to you, whatever it is, you always feel, think, and act as if there were a meaningful lesson in it all. When you do this, you are thinking and acting as programmed by the Western Tarot's fool in school archetype.

Archetypal Books

To summarize, now you know that society socializes children through myth, legend, and story, with an old energy archetype system. This old energy archetype system answers big questions, organizes thinking, and influences actions. You also know the old energy system is represented in the major arcana/archetype cards of the Western tarot system.

At this point, you might reasonably ask the question, "Why are *old energy* archetypes organized into the Western tarot?" The answer to that question comes in two parts. Part one of the answer is that it is easier to disseminate old energy archetypes when they are collected and neatly organized. Part two of the answer is that organizing them together makes the old energy archetype system (any archetype system really) a lot more powerful. Archetypes become more powerful when they are brought together because when they are brought together, they mingle, coalesce, and develop "deeper" and higher meaning. This is not because of any magical process; it is simply because that is how humans think.[12] Humans are evolutionarily programmed to search for deep meaning in things, and that is exactly what they do. Putting individually meaningful cards together facilitates the natural and spiritual search for deeper meaning in things.

Creation Templates

For your information, when you draw archetypes together in this fashion, i.e., when you collect and organize them into a single container, you create a book of archetypes, with each archetype being like a chapter in the book. [13] Each chapter (each card)

---

[12] Michael Sharp and Gina Sharp, "What Does It Mean to Be Human: Abraham Maslow and His Hierarchies of Need," Academia.edu.

[13] Note that a book of archetypes can be other than text and images of a tarot deck. A record album or art series may also provide an archetypal book. An example from my mind is the band Klaatu and their five albums. Their albums present, in the contracted shorthand of poetry set to music, a series of new energy archetypes.

In my view, Klaatu provided, back in the 1970s, as close to a new energy creation template as had been yet elaborates a specific archetypal idea. When you gaze at all the chapters in the book, you receive a "higher" meaning and message, just like you would if you read a traditional book. You do this, i.e., you collect archetypes together into a book, because it is easier to disseminate, and because doing so helps create deeper and higher meaning.

Recall at this point that archetypes do three things. They a) provide answers to big questions, b) organize how we think about the world and, c) guide/determine our actions. When you put a bunch of archetypes together into a book, when these archetypes comingle and coalesce into higher meanings that impact thought, action, and reality, and when you do that on purpose and with the express intent of controlling reality by influencing how people think and act, you create what I'd like to call a **Creation Template**. *A creation template is a powerful and carefully engineered collection of*

---

produced. Of course, Klaatu is not the only band to provide archetypes. Everybody from Katy Perry to Michael Jackson works with archetypes, either unconsciously or consciously.

archetypes developed to deliberately influence and control reality.[14]

At this point, it should not be hard to accept this truth, and it should not be hard to see that the Western Tarot is a creation template. You have already accepted the fact that archetypes can govern thinking and guide action. You have already accepted that drawing them together into a container provides higher meaning. At this point, the notion that you can organize archetypes into a creation template used to control reality should be an easy step forward to make. It is not magic. It is just human psychology. As we already know, archetypes provide answers to big questions, organize how we see and think about the world, and guide/determine our actions and reactions. When you deliberately put archetypes together into a book of archetypes designed to influence and control reality, you create a creation template.

The idea that a creation template controls reality by influencing the thoughts and actions of the people (or the planet) that accept it is expressed visually in the TOSAS **World** card (page over). In that card, the meniscus that surrounds the Earth represents a

---

[14] https://spiritwiki.lightningpath.org/Creation_Template.

creation template. The creation template forms the ground upon which we create physical reality. The twenty-four figures represent the rainbow spectrum of humanity creating the World while "standing" on the archetypal structure provided by the creation template. The planet in the middle is the result of the creation template materialized through the hands of the people of the world.

THE WORLD

Origin of the Templates

In the previous section, I said that creation templates are not magic, they are simply psychological engineering. That is true, but in a very real way, creation templates are also magic. If we define magic as the art and science of causing change to occur in conformity with will, without necessarily having to engage in actual physical force,[15] then by that definition, creation templates are definitely magic, because creation templates do just that. If I present you with a creation template that I have designed, and if you absorb that creation template, that creation template will then influence your thoughts and actions in the world. If I manage to influence your thoughts and actions with my

---

[15] Aleister Crowley(1875-1947) provides this definition of magic. Crowley, author of the Thoth Tarot Deck, is taken by some to be a wise and magical guy, a prophet, for a new aeon of "man" (sic). Personally, I see him as a man with serious psychological and emotional issues. He experienced child abuse, was assaulted by priests, and by fourteen was so messed up that, by his account, he butchered a cat. Whether his account is true or just twisted imagination doesn't matter. Either way, he is displaying serious emotional damage. I quote him regretfully because he has the best definition of magic around.

creation template, I am causing things to occur in conformity with my will. If I do that, I am engaged in creation magic using a creation template.

If that scares you a little bit, it should. You can pack a lot of power into a perfectly piquant creation template. That is not an argument not to use creation templates. If you want to get right down to it, Creation Templates drive the final stages of a planet's evolution.

If what I am saying about creation templates and the magical manipulation of reality is true, then as an awakening and activating citizen of Earth, you personally need to know what these things are, where they came from, and how to keep them under control.

With that frame in mind, an obvious question to ask at this point is, "Where do creation templates come from?" In answering that question, I first have to say, archetypes and creation templates do not just appear like magic. That is, they do not bubble up from some dank Jungian pool. Neither are they, as the early Freemasons who used the tarot deck to inscribe a creation template suggested,[16] given to us

---

[16] For a detailed historical look at the history of the Western Tarot, and the Freemason's important role, see

by God and Gods. Like all things of this world (some of which we may be proud of and some, not so much), archetypes and creation templates are

a) Designed by human minds and
b) Implemented for human purposes.

Of course, if archetypes are designed by human minds and implemented for human purposes, the next questions become a) what humans designed them and b) for what purposes did they do that.

Unfortunately, the answer to the questions of "what humans made them the template"[17] and "Why did they did so"[18] are to complicated to get into here. Here let me just say a few things relevant to our archetype study, starting with the fact that there are currently two basic creation templates active in this world, with two diametrically opposed purposes. There is currently, in my view, a dominant and

---

Mike Sosteric, "A Sociology of Tarot," *Canadian Journal of Sociology* 39, no. 3 (2014).

[17] Hint: it was ancient Sasanian priests. See my "From Zoroaster to Star Wars, Jesus to Marx: The Science and Technology of Mass Human Behaviour," https://www.academia.edu/34504691.

[18] Hint: they did it to build human civilization. See ibid.

highly toxic **old energy creation template**,[19] and a nascent and emerging **new energy creation template.**[20]

Old Energy Template

As for the old energy creation templates, it is a creation template built upon **old energy archetypes**.[21] As J. Harold Ellens says, old energy archetypes are archetypes and ideas of hierarchy, authority, exclusion, judgment, punishment (euphemized as "justice"), elitism, and rejection.[22] As I say, the energy that is generated when these archetypes are dominant in consciousness is imbalanced (prevalence of yang/**force**), violent, hierarchical, dominating, exclusionary, elitist, and in the most extreme cases, psychopathic. The reality that emerges from the energy and actions generated by

---

[19] For more on the old energy creation template, see https://spiritwiki.lightningpath.org/OECT.

[20] https://spiritwiki.lightningpath.org/NECT.

[21] http://spiritwiki.lightningpath.org/Old_Energy_Archetypes.

[22] J. Harold Ellens, "Introduction: The Destructive Power of Religion," in *The Destructive Power of Religion: Violence in Judaism, Christianity, and Islam*, ed. J. Harold Ellens(Westport, CT: Praegar, 2001).

these old energy archetypes is the same, which is to say, imbalanced (prevalence of yang/force), violent, hierarchical, dominating, exclusionary, elitist, and in the most extreme cases, psychopathic.[23]

If you are familiar with the Western Tarot, you can tell you have an old energy tarot deck in your hand by the presence of several "giveaway" cards. If the deck contains one or more of the Fool, Hierophant, Emperor, Empress, Devil, or Judgment cards, it is an old energy deck with old energy ideas of hierarchy, judgment, and punishment. If the accompanying commentary speaks of hierarchy, exclusion, punishment (euphemized as judgment),

---

[23] For your information, old energy archetypes and the old energy creation template into which they are organized developed roughly between -4,000 B.C. and 300 A.D. in the Fertile Crescent, concurrent with the rise of human civilization. Elite Sassanian priests arguably created the first creation template when, bringing together ancient ideas prevalent at the time, they they "wrote it all down" to support the agenda of their elite bosses. These ideas were then transmitted down through the ages, "rediscovered" here, enshrined as "scripture" there, throughout the world. The Western Tarot, which I have already introduced, is one example in a long line of more or less successful, and more or less sophisticated, implementations of this ancient old energy creation template.

and the salutatory benefits of suffering, it is an old energy deck implementing an old energy creation template.

The Old Energy Rider-Waite Tarot

For those familiar with the Western tarot, the Rider-Waite Tarot deck, created by the Freemason A.E. Waite,[24] is a powerful and pervasive implementation of the old energy creation template. I draw this conclusion based on my own research where I discovered that the Western esoteric tarot system, of which the Rider-Waite deck is the quintessential expression, is actually a deck created by political and economic elites hanging out in the exclusive Freemason lodges that popped up on the British Isle during the System's transition from Feudalism to Capitalism.[25] To make a long story short, the elites of the time adapted the proto-Iranian creation template, the old energy creation template, to new

---

[24] It may come as a surprise to many who use the Rider-Waite tarot for spiritual, divination, or healing services, but A.E. Waite was a devoted Freemason and the deck developed is, consequently, a masonic deck through and through.

[25] For the full story of the tarot, see my article Sosteric, "A Sociology of Tarot."

political and economic realities that were emerging at the time. They impregnated the "updated" template into Italian tarot cards, which they just "happened" to find lying around at the time, and then used those cards to distribute the archetypes, both internally to members, with hidden/esoteric meanings, and externally to the masses, with exoteric/"revealed" messages.[26]

I do not want to spend too much time on all that here. Let me just say, development of what we might appropriately call the **Masonic Old Energy Creation Template** culminated in the Rider-Waite tarot deck. The Rider-Waite deck was the notable work of notable Freemason A.E. Waite.

At this point, I will not say much more about the old energy creation template. I pick up a discussion in *Triumph of Spirit Book Two: Old and New Energy*

---

[26] Interestingly, they make no denial of this claim, and actually use it as a point of pride. In a book first published in 1888, S.L. MacGregor Mathers calls the cards "most ancient", as he enthusiastically, an erroneously, links them to illustrious locations like the "Temple of Ptah at Memphis." See S. L. MacGregor Mathers, *The Tarot: A Short Treatise on Reading Cards*(Samuel Weiser, 1993).

Archetypes. [27] From this point on, I will focus on the new energy creation template as provided by the Triumph of Spirit Archetype System (TOSAS).

New Energy Templates

Up until quite recently, all creation templates were old energy, and all tarot decks were based on the Rider-Waite old energy template. Some (mostly unconscious) attempts have been made to break free of old energy templates, but owing largely to...

a) Intentional obfuscation of the true nature of a tarot deck (i.e., it is a book of archetypes that forms a creation template),
b) The absence of any clear understanding of ancient old energy archetypes, and
c) The lack of any authentic, clear, and precisely specified alternative,

...attempts to break with the old energy system are underdeveloped, poorly implemented, and hobbled at the post.

---

[27] Michael Sharp, *The Triumph of Spirit Book Two: Old and New Energy Archetypes*, Triumph of Spirit (St. Albert: Lightning Path Press, 2017).

As you will now understand, this book and the other books in the TOSAS series, and the accompanying archetype cards represent a conscious and systematic break with ancient old energy creation templates. As you will see once you begin your study, and in stark contrast to the ancient old energy creation template which is violent, exclusionary, and elitist,[28] new energy archetypes in the TOSAS new energy creation template reflect ideas of balance, equanimity, equality, unity, empowerment, connection, emancipation, forgiveness, and utopia. Further, unlike the old energy creation template which goes to create a global reality of power, hierarchy, and privilege, the new energy creation template goes to create a reality of healing, equality, justice (not to be confused with punishment), emancipation, unity, connection (to Consciousness) and joy.

You can tell a new energy creation template, and a new energy archetype deck, if it is absent of a Fool and other "giveaway" cards and contains ideas like emancipation, realization, healing, awakening, unity, empowerment, joy, bliss, and so on.

---

[28] Ellens, "Introduction: The Destructive Power of Religion."

HEALING AND
SPIRITUAL PRACTICE

Now that you understand exactly what an archetype deck is, now that you know what a creation template is, now that you know where these creation templates come from,[29] and now that you can distinguish between old energy and new energy creation templates, you can move forward with your study and use of the Triumph of Spirit Archetype System (TOSAS).

People practice with archetype/tarot decks for one of several reasons. They use them for divination, healing, spiritual, psychological, and even initiatory work.[30] This is the same with the TOSAS. You can

---

[29] Reminder: they come from human minds and are implemented by human hands.

[30] At this point, you may be wisely questioning the wisdom of using a deck rooted in old energy archetypes as a prop for spiritual or psychological practice. If so, good! If your goal is spiritual awakening, activation, and connection, old energy decks will not help. Old energy decks were created to propagate an old energy creation template, not to help realize full human potential. Just as you cannot use a hammer to cut a piece of wood neatly, you cannot use an old energy tarot deck for authentic spiritual practice.

use it for divination and for spiritual, healing, psychological, and initiatory work. Note, however, that because the TOSAS does not currently include a set of minor arcana, its focus is primarily on healing, spiritual, and initiatory work. That said, you could still use the TOSAS cards for classic divination. To bring the powerful and transformative energies of the TOSAS into your standard practices, simply use the TOSAS cards in conjunction with other decks in your toolkit.

For your information, the healing and spiritual work you will do with this book is essentially about awakening, activation, and ascension. Through the powerful new energy archetypes cards, and the textual commentary contained herein, the new energy archetypes will help you

- Awaken to the truth of yourself and the world around you.
- Clear the dust and detritus of old energy archetypes that limit you.
- Empower you psychologically, emotionally, and spiritually.
- Make a better spiritual connection to your own soul/higher Self.

Attention Healers

When I say this deck is focused on healing work, I certainly mean that. This deck will help you heal yourself, but it can also help you heal others as well. It does this by acting as a spiritually sophisticated *assessment tool.* The TOSAS gives you the tools you need to help yourself or your clients a) **identify** ideas, behaviors, and environments that block, disconnect, and diminish, and b) **change** these ideas, behaviors, and environments so that they can better heal, awaken, activate, and connect.[31]

Of course, remember, it is always up to the individual whether they want to heal or not. Out of doubt, confusion, and fear, some people deny their realities and resist healing, even if they are actively seeking it out. If you do deal with people who deny and resist, do not wag your finger in judgment. Instead, simply remind them of the natural consequences of their actions, and let them make their own decisions.

---

[31] On the LP, we call this establishing right thought, right action, and right environment. Thus, this deck can you help you and your clients establish right thought, right environment, and right action.

It works something like this: as any doctor will tell you, if a person eats a diet high in fat, sugar, and processed foods, they will develop chronic and degenerative diseases, and eventually die. If they wish, they can continue to eat diets high in processed fats and sugars; however, the consequences of their poor diet (heart disease, etc.) fall primarily to them, those whom they love, and those that love them.

It is the same with archetypes and creation templates. Thinking with toxic old energy creation templates, remaining in the toxic environments created by these templates, and acting in toxic ways (what on the LP we call wrong thought, wrong environment, and wrong action), will lead clients on a downward spiral towards physical, emotional, psychological, and spiritual dysfunction. If they wish, they can continue to think with toxic ideas, live in toxic environments, and act out in toxic ways. If that is what they choose, that is fine. That is their choice. Do not judge. Simply remind them (and yourself) there are natural consequences for their choices. [32]

---

[32] For a glimpse at the impact of toxic environments, and the many unfortunate psychological, emotional, and physical consequences of toxic environments, see my

Getting started

To get started, first learn the meaning of the cards. To learn the meanings of the cards, read the entire book at least once. Then, focus on a specific card. Focus first on the specific heading, then read and understand the **symbolism**. Read the **description** to advance your understanding. To get a general idea of the assessment meaning, read the **upright**, **reversed** and **alignment** sections.

If you are engaged in LP activation study[33] and have the other Triumph of Spirit resources, read those through as well.

To begin an assessment

Mark your assessment space as sacred. You can look at the deck and browse it whenever you want; however, an **assessment**/reading (whether yours or someone else's) should be considered sacred. Mark your space as sacred in whatever way you like. Set an altar, light a candle or two, or whatever. If you are

---

article Mike Sosteric, "Toxic Socialization," *Socjourn* (2016).

[33] https://www.lightningpath.org/activate/.

not big on ceremony, as I am not, a simple intent/mantra statement is sufficient. Something like...

"For the highest good of all."

... will do.

If you are doing an assessment for yourself, recite the mantra as you shuffle the cards. If you are doing an assessment for another, have them recite the mantra as they cut/shuffle the cards.

General Guidance

When assessing for another, always explain the particular focus of the Triumph of Spirit deck <u>before</u> bringing it into your assessment/healing space. Say something like

This deck I am about to use is focused on emotional and psychological healing, and spiritual awakening and activation. Using this deck may trigger uncomfortable memories, insights, and realizations that require action and intervention. I may be able to help you with some of it, but if you have difficulties, get

additional support and guidance from
reputable professionals.

The above quotation is supplied as a card in the printed deck. If you prefer, you may show the supplied card "Lightning Strike" card. If your clients ask about "The Lightning Strike", say that the lightning strike is a brilliant stroke of insight and realization that leads to insight, healing, transformation, and even enlightenment.

When assessing yourself, do not overdo it. Although you can do as many assessments for others as you are capable, do no more than one a week for yourself. Better yet, do an assessment for yourself only when called. Otherwise, you will find the energy and power of the cards is dispersed.

Always remember, this is a powerful deck and individuals should always know what they are getting into when they use it, not only for their sake, but for yours as well. Being explicit and open about what you are up to builds trust and helps the client make informed choices, the consequences of which they cannot lay at your feet.

Expanding your Connection

To do a proper assessment for yourself or another, be sure to expand your connection to Consciousness as you begin. *When you are starting out, expand your connection only in calm, relaxed, and safe environments.* To facilitate connection, draw and enforce boundaries (e.g., place a cocoon of light around your body, and the body of your client), take deep breaths, and slow down.[34] When you are calm, open, and slow, visualize a bolt of light flashing down into your brain. Take a final deep breath and begin.

Read the card summaries and study the associated images. Let your training, expertise, and intuitive inner wisdom, flow.

If you are engaged in personal assessment or personal study, do not limit yourself to the temporal location of the assessment. If you remain open and receptive, insights may pop into your head hours and even days following a sacred spread.

---

[34] If you are highly sensitive, avoid caffeine and other harsher stimulants in periods immediately preceding your reading. Of course, if you are highly sensitive, it is probably best to avoid harsh stimulants at all times.

Spreading the Cards

When you have marked your assessment space as sacred with an intent statement, and when you have paused to expand your connection, shuffle and cut the cards in whatever manner you choose. As you are cutting and shuffling, ask yourself a specific question, like "Why am I here?", "What's blocking me?", "What do I need help with?", or something similar. If you are doing work for a client assessment, ask them to state their question aloud, because it makes the assessment easier. If they do not want to state their question aloud, that is fine to.

Just before you (or your client) lays the cards on the table, determine if you prefer a one or a three card spread. When you have determined the spread, lay the cards out. **If you are using the LP app,**[35] select a one or three card spread as per the client's choice, hand them the device, have them recite the mantra, and then instruct them to tap or shake the device.

For your information, a **one-card spread** is a single card placed on the table. The single card focuses attention on a specific idea, action, reaction, or environment relevant to the client's concerns or

---

[35] https://www.lightningpath.org/lp-app/

issues. **A three-card spread** represents a more complex view of concerns or issues, with a specific focus on supports and resistances. The three card spread looks like this:

A Q A

In a three-card spread, the card in the middle represents you or your client, the issue, the blockage, the environment, etc. It is the querent, query, or **Q-card**. The cards on the left and right are **alignments.** Alignments represent past, present, and potential emotional, psychological, spiritual, or physical realities, personal or collective. When alignment cards are upright, they usually represent positive and supportive things, conducive to forward movement, and encouraging of mental health. When alignment cards are reversed, they may be negative and undermining, presenting obstacles to forward movement, and encouraging anxiety, stress, and disease at all levels. Note, an upright card may find itself negatively aligned, indicating difficulties, challenges, oppression, and such.

More specifically, in a three-card spread, the *card behind* (i.e. the card to the left) represents influences that support and lift or, if reversed, create drag, drip toxicity, hamper progress, etc. The card in front (i.e., the card to the right) represents things that pull

43

the client forward or, if reversed, suppress and oppress. Note that identifying negative alignments is not a judgment leading to punishment; it is an opportunity for correction and forward movement.

Assessment

The hardest part of reading the cards is synthesizing the information into an assessment. Doing a proper assessment is a complicated and involved task that I cannot go into here. However, a few general comments are in order.

To do a proper assessment, you need to understand the cards, be intuitively open, and be professionally skilled.

Note, past professional training is relevant, so do not be shy about drawing on your professional psychological, psychiatric, or other training.

Finally, keep in mind, the TOSAS system is embedded in the larger spiritual and intellectual context of the Lightning Path. For more Lightning Path, visit https://www.lightningpath.org/. For training aimed specifically at TOSAS assessment, https://www.lightningpath.org/shop/instruction/.

Attention LP Students

As LP students learn, spirituality is about connecting your bodily consciousness to your highest Consciousness.[36] Spiritual systems are systems of thought designed to teach you how to connect. Spiritual practices are practices designed to help you make a connection to Consciousness. Spiritual tools are tools designed facilitate and support connection.

You can use the TOSAS system as a spiritual tool to facilitate awakening, activation, and eventually, connection, because that is what it was designed for. It was designed to help you make a safe and pure spiritual connection.

As a spiritual aspirant after stronger and higher connection, you use the TOSAS in a beginner, intermediate, and advanced way.

When you use the cards at a beginner/awakening level, you are using them to help you awaken to your realities and heal from any damage you incurred.

---

[36] Michael Sharp, *The Rocket Scientists' Guide to Authentic Spirituality* (St. Albert, Alberta: Lightning Path Press, 2010).

When used at an intermediate/activation level, you are using the cards to remove old energy archetypes and replace them with new energy archetypes.

When used at an advance/ascension level, you use the cards as "channels" of connection through which you access pure new energies.

This book is focused on the beginner/awakening aspect of your study, although some intermediate and advanced elements are introduced here as well.

To use this book to help you awaken and heal, read through the entire book at least once, and then study cards individually after that.

To study cards individually,

First, state this mantra.

I want the truth and nothing but the truth, no compromise and no strings attached.

Second, pick a card that attracts your eye, or shuffle, cut, and pick the top card.

Third, learn the title.

Fourth, note and memorize the **key phrase**.

Fifth, learn the symbolism. The symbolism is explained in the symbolism paragraph. Don't rush through. Spend a moment or two on each sentence to make sure the meaning finds its way through.

Sixth, read the narrative. The narrative is the new energy "story" being told by the card. For example, the card Joyful is the story not of spiritual servitude and tutelage, but of your glorious and joyful incarnation.

Seventh, when you understand the narrative, read the "assessment" sections for healing and awakening insights.

Remember, do not rush through the descriptions. Take a moment or to **grok**[37] each sentence and section.

Also, when you first go through this deck, it is best to keep a single card with you for a few days. While it is with you (i.e., in your purse, on your phone, etc.), continue to recite the memorized key phrase, read over the text, think about the symbolism, etc. During this process, try and keep yourself open to

---

[37] The word grok (literally "to drink") is a word coined by science fiction writer Robert A. Heinlein in his book *Stranger in a Strange Land* to indicate deep understanding.

ideas and connections between the archetype and your own life. But, be discerning.[38]

Have an open mind, just don't be an airhead.

Not every connection you make, nor every insight that flashes, is meaningful or worthwhile. Because of the old energy archetypes implanted in us as children, and all the media reinforcement that goes on, some of the stuff that pops into your mind might be pure crap. Especially at the beginning, be careful. If you notice hatred, anger, hierarchy, violence, judgment, punishment, exclusion, guilt, shame, and things like that in your understandings and insights, something is off. Always keep your thoughts positive and inclusive by practicing good mental hygiene. Learn to control all of your body's thoughts, and reject those that are unworthy of your **joyful**, **powerful**, and **masterful** spiritual status.

Finally, at the start, I would not recommend you spend more than 45 minutes in any single session with any individual. Give yourself time and space to process, integrate, and ground things. If you move too fast, you will either spin your wheels in the

---

[38] For guidance on discernment, see Michael Sharp, *The Rocket Scientists' Guide to Spiritual Discernment* (St. Albert, Alberta: Lightning Path Press, 2011).

48

ground or be overwhelmed by new information and new perspectives. Trust your gut on this. If you find yourself being confused and overwhelmed, step away for a few days.

THE ARCHETYPES

Overview

In the rest of the book, you will find all the new energy archetype cards in the Triumph of Spirit archetype deck listed and described. Each of the entries follows a specific format with headings that are self-explanatory.

For your reference, italicized text marks advanced ideas.

Bold text indicates ideas that are important and that you need know, lightning Path terminology mentioned for the first time (e.g. **new energy**), and *TOSAS archetypes*. For example, the sentence "We lift physical creation towards Consciousness so that another **world** may **graduate** and be **reborn**" refers to three archetypes in the Triumph of Spirit lexicon, World, Rebirth, and Graduation.

When you see a word or a phrase in bold or italic, pause for a moment or two to make sure you understand the idea, and transfer the word or phrase into memory. [39]

---

[39] I find it takes about two minutes to transfer something that is relatively familiar from short term to long-term memory. It takes longer and requires more effort to transfer unfamiliar things, like new words and concepts.

Now, without further ado, I give you the Triumph of Spirit archetype system.

IDENTITY

JOYFUL

Joyful

Key Phrase: Joyful in Manifestation.

Symbolism: A Joyful soul walking the yellow brick road into manifestation. The fractal blue waters of creation support the figure and the road. A beam of light shows a strong connection to Source Consciousness. Seven chakras support the body (and **the Body**).[40] The road emerges from the crown chakra Consciousness of the figure, indicating that the individual soul constructs its own path into incarnation. Before the figure lies the vast untapped potential of creation.

Narrative: This card teaches us about our identity and creative journey. This card answers the questions "Who am I?" and "Where am I going?"

At the highest level, we are sparks of creator Consciousness on a joyful creative journey. This is the beginning of the journey of our Soul as it enters into a physical body to accomplish the **Great Work**. As a member of the glorious family of Spirit, we are **joyful**, **masterful**, and **powerful**. Embracing light, life, and connection, we descend into physical

---

[40] http://spiritwiki.lightningpath.org/Waters_of_Creation and http://spiritwiki.lightningpath.org/The_Body.

creation, **sacrificing** so that we might uplift and enjoy physical creation.

At mundane levels, this is a journey. This journey involves physical, psychological, emotional, or spiritual movement. *Physically*, this is a pilgrimage or a move. *Psychologically*, this is the journey to self-awareness, identity, enlightenment, and purpose. *Spiritually*, this is the journey to Connection (the journey back home). *Emotionally*, this is the journey to emotional maturity, health, and healing.

Present in an assessment upright, physically, psychologically, spiritually, and emotionally, you are willing to undertake the journey, or you are already on your way towards healing, activation, and connection. There is lots of work, but if you stay motivated and alert, seek guidance and accept assistance, you will make good progress forward. You have what it takes to travel the Path.

Card reversed and/or negatively aligned, there are feelings of unworthiness and incompetence, fear and misunderstanding. Unable to move past fear and resistance, you fail to consider the consequences of inaction. Shocked by what we have done in the past, you recoil, aghast at the horror. Ignoring the reality that surrounds you, you are mired in the muck of complacency. You miss a great opportunity. Disappointment, regret, and depression lie ahead.

Alignments indicate support and obstacles to realizing our identity and true self. *Positive alignments* indicate friends, family, co-workers, and life situations that support our exploration, and support who we truly are. *Negative alignments* indicate sources of resistance and blockage, naivety, foolishness, indoctrination, and servitude to the ideas of others. The time to explore our identity and true Self has come, but fear, external resistance, confusion, doubt, low self-esteem, or something else, prevents us from taking a closer look. Alternatively, we are frightened by what we see, or are moving way too fast. Impatience causes instability. Instability hampers advancement. We make mistakes. Accidents abound.

This journey is necessary. Expansion, (spiritual, emotional, psychological, etc.) growth, evolution, and achievement lie ahead, but only if you take the first step, and see whom you are. As with all journeys, work is involved. You may refuse if you wish; but wrong choice leads inevitably to the diminishment of soul and death of the body. Avoid that fate. Gather **strength** and move forward.

AWAKENING

THE CALLING

The Calling

Key Phrase: It is time to wake up.

Symbolism: Consciousness/Spirit is calling. Consciousness descends from the Crown and pulls the **bodily ego** upward. A powerful pull. An irresistible push. An unignorable call to awaken. The figures, representing the bodily ego, look up as they respond to the Call. The body/mind begins to awaken. It is time to take the journey home.

Narrative: This card represents the call to awaken *and* our response to this call. *There is more to this life than at first seems.* The search for greater meaning and purpose begins. The powerful urge to embrace truth and reality grows. We take our first step and move forward on the Path.

At the highest level, this is the call to **awaken** to identity/purpose, **activate**, and eventually **ascend** to a higher state. We understand there is a need to move forward. We throw off the blindfold and begin to awaken in a measure that we are able to handle.

At mundane levels, this is a push forward towards insight and awareness. We have a problem, but the solution is there. If we pay closer attention, if we listen to inner guidance, and if we trust our intuition, the solution is right there to hand.

Present in an assessment upright, this card represents the call to awaken. This is the rising suspicion that something is wrong, that something is missing, and that something needs to be done. This is a push to move forward. Responding to the call, you begin to see through the thin veneer of fantasy and self-delusion. You begin to awaken. Insight and understanding begin to grow. Vision clears. Awareness slowly dawns. Perhaps for the first time since birth, you see the truth of things.

Card reversed and/or negatively aligned, this is an oppressive force of violence, pain, corruption, deception, disruption, confusion, subjugation, and immobilization. The call to awaken grows, pressure builds inside, but resistance to the call is profound. Overwhelmed by fear, confusion, low self-worth, social convention, autocracy, external resistance, violence, etc., you suppress the call and lash out. Anger boils within and rots you deep inside.

Alignments indicate supports and obstacles to awakening. *Positive alignments* indicate a strong call to awaken and the presence of support and wise guidance. No longer a subtle sensibility, no longer a gentle touch, an intense sense of urgency rises inside us. *Negative alignments* indicate uncertainty, confusion, psychological or emotional resistance, and external judgment and control. The call should lead to awakening, understanding, and transformation, but something, or someone, blocks the way forward. We feel judged and unworthy. We believe the lies they have told. We succumb to the **Great Deception** and submit. We lower our heads and turn away from our own highest Light.

Understand, nobody is here to judge and condemn. The calling leads to insight, enlightenment, **emancipation,** em**power**ment, and **connection**, not judgment and damnation. Who wants to live in the dull grey of normal? Gather your gumption. Release your attachments to drama and toxicity. Let go of anger and negativity. The key to moving forward is conscious intent. Say, "I wish to awaken; I wish to move forward." Stay focused on the Path before you. Be wary of obstacles. Pay attention to challenges. Be mindful of that which surrounds you. Find the ones who have your best interests at heart. Move! It is important. As the planet ascends, the physical, emotional, and psychological consequences of disconnection will rapidly manifest.

THE MASTER

The Master

Key Phrase: The master within.

Symbolism: The physical unit is mature, healthy, and strong. The Soul has arrived. United as one, they manifest and control physical creation. Lemniscate below and above, a strong connection keeps everything properly aligned. The figure stands tall and is confident and proud. Palm pointed up, palm pointed down, the master implements the Divine Plan. Highest Self united with self. **Bodily Ego** merged with **Spiritual Ego** and aligned. That which is in Consciousness above reflected perfectly in matter below.

Narrative: This archetype teaches us of our mastery. Please understand, this is not your first time in a body and not your first act in the show. You have **joyfully** incarnated many times before. Through countless incarnations you have mastered your many skills. Know this. You are not a fool in a cosmic school. You are a **powerful** and **joyful master**, a **star** here to uplift and ascend creation.

At the highest level, this is us incarnated in a **powerful** and connected physical unit. We are not now nor have we ever been "fools in school." We are not here to submit to the will of others. We are not here to "learn your lessons." We are not here to "find our place" in the castes and classes of this world. On the contrary, we are masters of creation with lifetimes of training and experience. We have a special purpose and we are here to implement a special plan.

At mundane levels, this is our personal and professional mastery. This is certainly not onerous and odoriferous work. This is what we are trained for. This is what we are good at. This is what comes easy for us.

Present in an assessment upright, this card represents self-confidence, expertise, focus, will, mastery, and commitment to manifesting the Plan. Knowing who you are and why you came, you are ready and willing to get the job done. Focused and confident, you do the things that you need to do to move yourself and your life forward. Accepting there is more to life than money, sex, and power, you find true purpose and embrace your mastery.

Card reversed and/or negatively aligned, this card indicates family/work/social toxicity, and pervasive psychological distress/disorder. Family enmeshes and restrains. Coworkers make unreasonable demands. Employers command and control. Governments steal and assault. Those threatened by your progress drag you down. Your own will and desire trumped by the authority of others. Darkness and dysfunction surround.

Alignments indicate people, environments, and thoughts that support or undermine your mastery. *Positive alignments* indicate positive progress and support. *Negative alignments* indicate indolence, vacillation, equivocation, etc. Blockage keep you down. Low self-esteem, lack of confidence, reduced self-efficacy, etc. prevent you from stepping up. There is work that you need to do, but you are unaware or feel powerless. You doubt your ability, intelligence, competence, and mastery. You believe yourself talentless, skill-less, and worthless. You rely exclusively on external expertise and authority to tell you what to do. You please people in order to fit in.

When connected and properly aligned, your life is an easy breezy reflection of divine higher Consciousness. When healthy and fully functioning, you are a master at manifesting will. Remember, you are no "fool in school." Be confident and proud of your **joyful** self. The goal is **alignment** with your highest Self, and expression/**connection** to the **master** that is within. Always remember, you are a **master** manifesting Divine will.

THE WORLD

The World

Key Phrase: Our World. Our Work.

Symbolism: Twenty-four figures, symbolic of the twelve signs of the zodiac, the twelve tones of creation, the twelve rays of emanation, etc., circle and work with Gaia. All life participates. An unbreakable and inviolable meniscus isolates Earth and protects the universe from the fallout of an experimental creation. Work and purpose as we manifest the Divine Plan.

Narrative: This card teaches us about the Great Work. This card conveys the reason we are here. We are here as **joyful masters** of creation. We are here to implement **The Divine Plan**. We are here to evolve the planet. We are here to ascend the **world**.

At the highest level, this is the work of evolving and ascending another planet, a new pearl in the vast cosmic ocean of creation. You should know, this is a big job and it takes a long time. Furthermore, there are no bystanders in this process. All life forms, not only humans, are implicated in the process. Understand that to ascend, the effort of all life is required. Respect even the lowly worm because their work is as essential as yours is.

At a more mundane level, this is a job, a hobby, home, our family (it takes lots of work to maintain a family), our friendships, or anything else that requires work and attention to create and maintain.

Present in an assessment upright, this card represents business, the world, work, and even the Great Work. This is our profession, but not necessarily our job. This is the work that we *want* to do. This is the work that we came to do. Please note, there is no "I" in World. The Work is *always* teamwork. Even a writer writing alone in a room requires a team. Without a paper industry, a computer industry, and a retail industry, the writer writes only for self.

Card reversed and or negatively aligned, your purpose is venal and your groups are selfish and toxic. Spiritual/Divine purpose is submerged by greed and self-interest. You work for personal profit and gain. You work according to the will of another.

Alignments indicate people, environments, and thoughts that support or undermine your work. *Positive alignments* indicate understanding, acceptance, and support. You understand there is work to do, you realize you do not have to do it alone, and you see that help is available. Solipsism and fear give way to compassion, connection, and the unity of collective purpose. Self emerges in others around you and you rejoice. Your world begins to transform. *Negative alignments* indicate ideology and fear, low self-esteem, distraction, worry, uncertainty, and toxic friends, family, co-workers, and authority that surrounds you. The things around you drag you down. To avoid pain and anguish, you accept the **world** around you as it is. Giving up, you surrender to the will of others. You justify and excuse your behaviors. Higher Self recoils. Consciousness in the body declines.

You can live a life according to your own divine and **maste**rful purpose, or not. You can play as part of an ascension team, or pretend you are in this only for yourself. Note, a life lived according to another, or a life lived in solipsistic isolation, is no life at all. What keeps you isolated and alone? Who keeps you dazed and confused? Who keeps you silenced and in thrall? Who keeps you on your knees? Ask for answers and you shall receive. Learn the truth and a way forward will emerge. Remember you are a **joyful master**. Remember your purpose. Look forward to the **promise**. It is time to join with all life and awaken, activate, and ascend this physical **world**.

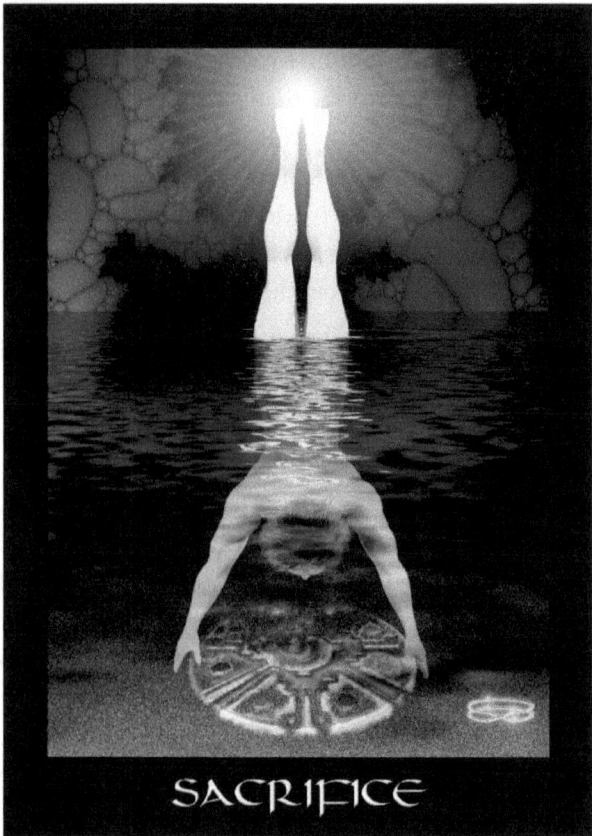

SACRIFICE

Sacrifice

Key Phrase: The sacrifice of disconnection.

Symbolism: Here we see a **joyful master** sacrificing connection to Consciousness in order to descend into **The Waters** (of Manifestation) and uplift physical creation (the earthen disk). Anchored by the light and glory of Consciousness/The Fabric, but submerged, inverted, and with no light at the Crown (chakra), she is disconnected. Embracing physical creation, she strains, struggles, and succeeds. She lifts physical creation up (ascends creation) through the darkness of in-animation towards the highest expressions of Consciousness.[41]

Narrative: This archetype teaches us of our sacrifice. We cannot deny, the Great Work is challenging and difficult. We accept this effort as a necessary sacrifice so that we might descend into physical manifestation in order to uplift all of creation.

At the highest levels, this is the sacrifice required to undertake the Great Work, which is the work of ascension. Disconnected and blindfolded, we

---

[41] For more on ascension, see Michael Sharp, *The Book of Life: Ascension and the Divine World Order.*

73

descend into darkness in order that we might ascend physical creation. It is hard work, the conditions are not ideal, and so we struggle and suffer. We accept and endure, for the reward of our effort is a pearl of inestimable value--an ascended and **graduated world**.

At mundane levels, these are the priorities we set and the sacrifices we make so that we can work and live the way we want. Remember, nothing good comes without work, effort, and sacrifice.

Present in an assessment upright, this card represents sacrifice, hard work, and effort. A goal has been set and you need to work hard to achieve it. Make sure your priorities are in place. Make sure you are committed to the Work. If priorities are in place and commitment is true, progress is tangible and steady. There may be challenges, but stay focused and a way forward is always available.

Card reversed and/or negatively aligned, you accept unnecessary suffering that is damaging to the physical unit and detrimental to the work you do. Violence and toxicity lead to physical, emotional, and psychological damage. You conflate abuse with sacrifice. You believe suffering is actually good for you. You have told yourself, what does not kill you makes you stronger; but it is not true. What does not kill you damages you, disconnects you, and leaves you scarred. Foolishly, you ignore the damage and accept the negative consequences as a necessary "cross" you must bear. Psychological and emotional damage accrue because of the violence and abuse you endure.

Alignments indicate people, environments, and thoughts that honor your sacrifices, or those who diminish and deride. *Positive alignments* indicate cooperative sacrifice and collective mission. We sacrifice together to achieve a goal. *Negative alignments* indicate reaction, defensiveness, avoidance of reality, repression and depression. Addictions (shopping, exercise, alcohol, tobacco, sugar, etc.) provide a psychological and emotional escape from suffering and pain. Indoctrination nails you to a cross and you suffer in silence and alone.

To change your life, change the way you think about many things, starting with your view of sacrifice. Understand, there is no psychological or emotional benefit to pain and suffering. In order to complete the Great Work, sacrifice may be required; but suffering, strife, and abuse are not requirements of the Work. Focus, hard work, and commitment are what drives creation forward. That is all.

THE PROMISE

The Promise

Key Phrase: The Garden of Connection.

Symbolism: Two figures rejoice in paradise. Bathed in the highest light of Consciousness/Christ/God (the Sun[42]), they stand firmly in the waters of manifestation. Having, through sacrifice and effort, uplifted the dense and inanimate disk of physical creation, they bask in the power and the glory of an ascended creation. This is purpose achieved. This is the goal realized. This is **graduation** and ascension. This is the promised reward.

Narrative: This card teaches us the point and the purpose of incarnation. This is why we strive for **mastery**. This is why we **joyfully** incarnate. This is why we struggle in duality. This is why we **sacrifice** and commit.

At the highest levels, this card represents the exaltation of Consciousness in matter. This is what drives us to enter incarnation. This is why we suffer the pains and the **sacrifice** of damnation. This is the

---

[42] Or, is it the Son? I am the Sun of God. I am the Son of God. It is the same thing I think, but since the word 'sun" is gender neutral, it is better. "We are the Sun of God".

end-point of planetary gestation. This is why we keep coming back. We are here to uplift and exalt creation with highest Consciousness so we can play in another Garden of Eden. It is the only job worth having, the best job worth doing, and we have all been down doing it for a long time. It is the promise of the power and the glory of Consciousness, descended and fully expressed in the Body, that keeps all of us down here coming back.

At mundane levels, this represents that which motivates our projects. Our wants and needs, whether healthy or no. This is, to name a few, the promise of shelter, the safety of family, the glory of love, the need for acceptance, the enjoyment of sex, and (sometimes) the lure of power and wealth. Whatever it is that drives us is present, here and in the alignments to this card.

Present in an assessment upright, this card represents clean and healthy motivations, pure vision, and the conscious desire to uplift and ascend. A vision of life and happiness is forming (or has already formed) in your mind, and you want to move forward towards that vision.

Card reversed and/or negatively aligned, this is a very negative card. Selfishness. Cruelty. Enslavement. Assault. Domination. Control.

Hierarchy. Power. Holocaust. What you desire is power, wealth, and control, and you will do anything you can to access it. You find your life drained of its joy and vitality. Energy is wasted. Pain and suffering abound. Drugs fill the voids.

Alignments indicate people, environments, and thoughts that support or undermine your vision and purpose. *Positive alignments* indicate clarity of vision and positive supports. You find your friends, family, and coworkers aligned with your vision and purpose. *Negative alignments* indicate perversion of motivation, selfishness, cruelty, holocaust, and attack. Those around you enable negativity and toxicity. At every turn, your vision is distorted and blocked. Paranoia sets in. Panic rises.

In the end, the horror show is a self-imposed illusion, taught to us as children. God's true promise is health, wealth, and paradise for all, right here and right now. This promise is not limited to a select group, or restricted to a few "worthy" ones. God's promise is for everybody. We all **joyfully** incarnate. We all make **sacrifices**. We all work on the **world**. We all deserve rest and reward. We all participate in the ascended utopia. Do not fear. Rejoice. In your darkest hour, this promise is a radiant beacon that lights your way home.

REALIZATION

Realization

Key Phrase: The mind's true liberation

Symbolism: The pearl-like globe embedded in purple energies indicates the involvement of the crown chakra. The yellow box is a box of constriction and limitation. The hand represents authority implemented through crown chakra control (i.e., mind control through ideology and archetypes). The ideas in our mind shape, bind, or emancipate. The hand of authority emerges through the mind and clutches the figure in the box, but the figure is breaking free. Another figure has already escaped. Striving for connection (looking up), she dips her foot in the new reality (the water) below. Moving forward, she rejoins all who are free.

Narrative: This card represents the mind's true liberation. This is the lightning flash of creative/intuitive/intellectual realization. This is powerful, electrical, inspiration as it electrifies physical manifestation and reverberates throughout creation.

At the highest level, we realize (or begin to realize) the truth of things. We have been lied to. We have been deceived. We are more than what we have been told. Breaking free from the limitations of mental slavery, we realize the truth. We accept the **sacrifice**. We remember the **promise**. We reclaim our status as a **joyful master** of creation. No longer confined, we work on the **world** to ascend/**graduate** our creation.

At mundane levels, this card represents a breakthrough. We tear down a wall. We break through a blockage or obstacle. We finally understand. Breaking free of control, error, familiarity, and limitation, we embrace diversity and pursue new energy alternatives and new energy solutions.

Present in an assessment upright, this card represents insight, realization, and enlightenment. We realize, or are close to realizing, a truth about our self, or our Self. We realize, or are close to realizing, a truth about our life or something in it. We are OK with what we see, even if it makes us uncomfortable. As understanding dawns, we move forward. Life begins to improve.

Card reversed and/or negatively aligned, this card indicates diversion, deception, confusion, misdirection, and deceit. An idea, or a person with an idea, holds you in a vice-like grip and prevents you from seeing the truth. Somebody has given you bad advice and you have foolishly, followed it. You are deluded and mentally oppressed. You are controlled. Your life is not your own. You are a robot.

Alignments indicate people, environments, and thoughts that support or undermine realization. *Positive alignments* indicate people and resources available to assist with realization or to guide us in understanding and direction. They push us forward with a gentle and loving touch. A little bird whispers in our ear. *Negative alignments* indicate deep confusion, delusion, self-delusion, and pervasive deception. Rigid fundamentalism restrains you with a vise-like grip. Fear, hatred, and self-loathing prevent you from removing your chains.

Moving forward you should know, realization is not a single event. We realize the truth in stages. We attain emotional and intellectual **emancipation** systematically and by "degrees." Examine your ideas carefully. Fact check what others are saying. Evaluate your behaviors. Do you know why you do certain things? Do not be trapped by somebody else's agenda. Facilitate forward movement through careful discernment and ongoing gentle realization.

INITIATION

Initiation

Key Phrase: The flesh no longer weak.

Symbolism: The chaos, darkness, disease, and death of old energy creation lie below. A figure climbing an activation spiral struggles out of the darkness. The ladder is vertical; the climb is difficult; the pitfalls numerous. However, there is hope. As we release fear, as we clarify and realize, **strength** returns. The pace accelerates. New energies begin to flow. A circle/energy sphere provides a boundary to protect the climber and keep her on track.

Narrative: This card represents initiation and ascent. This is a point of emotional, psychological, spiritual, and/or political maturation. This is, individually or collectively, another step up the ladder. We know who we are. We **realize** our purpose. We understand our **sacrifice**. We roll up our sleeves. Our connection improves. We ascend a little higher.

At the highest levels, this is the initiation of physical creation, the initiation of evolution, and the final initiation of Consciousness's descent into a willing and able (i.e. properly prepared) physical vessel.

When the **work** is complete, the spirit is willing and the flesh is no longer weak.

At mundane levels, this is the initiation of a project. This is the activity that follows the idea and the decision to build. A house. A screenplay. A business. A family.

Present in an assessment upright, this card represents the solidification of intent, the initiation of a plan, a step forward, or a new beginning. Doubt, fear, and confusion are gone. The pieces come together. You solve the puzzle. You are consciously ready to move forward. Strong and deliberate forward movement ensues. You get started and you start making things happen.

Card reversed and/or negatively aligned, this card indicates fear, hatred, anger, and confusion. Demons, devils, and dragons in mind keep you locked down. Toxic relationships at home, work, and in the "social" lodges suppress and control instead of uplift and emancipate. Feelings of rejection, dejection, and worthlessness abound. Deep self-doubt leads us to conform. We would rather fit in and follow than fly.

Alignments indicate people, environments, and thoughts that support forward movement towards connection/ascension, or that undermine us and drag us down. *Positive alignments* indicate positive support. The path ahead may be difficult and challenging, but thanks to available support, progress is possible. *Negative alignments* indicate negativity, suppression, and loss. You are beaten. Like a horse that finally submits, you are broken. Fear, violence, threat, confusion, and oppression have proven too much. You acquiesce and succumb. Self-delusion spreads like cancer.

At times, you may feel lost and defeated. Do not give up. Do not let depression overwhelm your bright Soul. Remember, the only loss that is a true loss is the loss that comes when you give up and stop trying. Remind yourself of the **promise**. Embrace **joyful mastery** and the **strength** of divine purpose. Bedraggled and abused, but breathing and alive all the same, there is still hope and there is still time. Do not succumb to hatred. Do not be afraid. Do not feel unworthy. Do not allow yourself to be damned. Out of the valley of the shadow of death, you may yet still emerge. It is a simple choice that you make to create the World where you live. Open to your own higher Consciousness. Trust in your own higher Self. Embrace and accept the lightning flash of your own highest inspiration. Listen to the calling. Find your way home.

ACTIVATION

STRENGTH

Strength

Key Phrase: Service to the Plan.

Symbolism: Gaia embodied as the tree of all life. Kneeling figure: An empowered, but humble servant of God, honoring Gaia, and willing to serve the **Divine Plan**. Gaia, charging for the task at hand, which is evolution of the Body in order to enable its full connection to Consciousness. Land, barren, grass, beginning to grow because of connection and purpose realized. The figure stands. Life bursts forth. Waters of manifestation, Waters of Consciousness, Waters of Creation. The Water feeds physical manifestation and nurtures the new Garden of high Consciousness emerging.

Narrative: This card represents true strength, which is not psychopathic domination and control of another, but the strength that comes from comprehension, awareness, connection, and service.

At the highest level, this is the strength that comes when you serve the Divine evolutionary plan to connect the Body (and the body) with higher Consciousness. You do not incarnate primarily for business or pleasure. You incarnate to uplift creation. You incarnate to actuate the Divine plan.

At mundane levels, this is the strength that you need to get through life. This is physical, psychological, emotional, and even spiritual strength, when applied to mundane tasks. Never doubt, you are strong. Never doubt, you have what it takes to get through.

Present in an assessment upright, this card represents true strength of mission and purpose. No longer should you sit in impotence and silence. No longer should you dominate and oppress others. Having **realized** the truth, move to embrace **power** and **promise**. Gather your **strength, joyfully** embrace your **mastery** and stand for what is right.

Cards reversed and/or negatively aligned, you struggle with social convention and social control. Low self-esteem and self-worth weaken you. Strength is confused with the domination of others. The bullying use of force stands in the place of true strength. Aggression obscures your pain. Bravado and violence conceal fundamental spiritual weakness.

Alignments indicate environments, people, and actions that support the growth/emergence of true strength, or that encourage violence, aggression, and domination of Self and others. *Positive alignments* indicate strong convictions, true purpose, and support all around. With strong alignments, limitations are shattered, strength is supported, and weakness dissipates. *Negative alignments* indicate selfish individuals, toxic environments, venal priorities, fear, hatred, arrogance, confusion, and other props of violence and disconnection. Stuck in the toxic mud of your dark and toxic world, you scramble and thrash. Lacking true strength, you lash out and harm others. Oppressing your own Self, you dominate others in the service of a venal plan. Impotent, you accept the toxicity that is. Blinded, you see no way out.

Understand this: violence and domination are not strength. Violence is the first and last resort of the weak and disconnected. The connected never express strength through the oppression and suppression of others, or of the Self. At the bleeding edge of human evolution, there is no contest; there is only global unity. True **power** and strength come after we align with our highest Self and commit to the Divine Plan. True power comes only when we work together as equals to fulfill the **promise** and the Plan. Embrace true purpose. Draw true strength. Evolve the body, exalt the planet, and **graduate** into universal, cosmic creation.

ALIGNMENT

Alignment

Key Phrase: Truth, responsibility, atonement.

Symbolism: An abstract representation of **alignment.**[43] A sword, balanced on either side by force and formation (yang and yin). A key offered to you by Jupiter, the planet of alignment. Not the sword of judgment, but the sword of alignment. The key to the Kingdom of God, the Kingdom of high Consciousness, which is Truth, responsibility, love, and atonement.

Narrative: This card teaches us the key to forward movement, activation, and **graduation**, which is alignment with our highest Self. Always remember, the physical unit is merely a vehicle for the Divine Sun of your Self. To move forward, align the thoughts and actions of your physical unit with your perfect, highest Self.

At the highest level, this is perfect alignment with Self, perfect alignment with the Consciousness of God, or the active pursuit thereof. Listen carefully.

---

[43] Alignment is a key LP concept. It refers to the ideal situation when the physical unit is properly oriented (i.e. aligned) with its higher, animating Consciousness. For more see http://spiritwiki.lightningpath.org/Alignment.

Alignment is not an onerous chore. Alignment does not bring pain, suffering, darkness, and disconnection. Alignment brings power, peace, joy, and the highest possible connection.

At mundane levels, this is healing and repair of the physical body. We put aside hypocrisy and self-delusion. We align our actions with our own best intentions. We breathe deep and **joyfully** atone for past "sin."[44] Focused on the manifestation of the **promise**, we fix that which is broken in this **world** and ourselves.

Present in an assessment upright, this represents the urge and drive to align, to move forward, clear up the issues, line up the pieces, and make the necessary changes (change jobs, direction, friends, etc.). You know who you are, you know why you are here, and you know what you need to do. Take action and align.

Card reversed and/or negatively aligned, this is fear, resistance, and failure to take responsibility. Powerful new energies flow, but you remain trapped in dysfunction. You resist accountability. You deny your actions and pretend you are without sin. You

---

[44] For the Lightning Path definition of "sin," see http://spiritwiki.lightningpath.org/Sin/.

embrace the great delusion. You fail to take action and align. You feel a painful burn rising inside.

Alignments indicate supports that help us face the truth and align behaviors, or resistances that encourage misalignment and disjuncture. *Positive alignments* indicate accountability, responsibility, and gathering support. We do not deny our sins, hide our mistakes, or make up excuses. We take responsibility, embrace error, fix what is broken, and return ourselves to alignment. *Negative alignments* indicate internal and external resistance to alignment. Enablers spin their toxic webs around us. Those who benefit from our servitude subvert and oppress. Judgment and shame keep us down. Emotional and psychological pressure to align and move forward builds.

For the truly woke, judgment and condemnation are passé. It is not about commandments, rules, or following orders. It is not about morality or divine assessment. It is not about enduring punishment. It is about aligning with highest Self, fully manifesting Divine vision, and being who you came here to be. To get from there to here, simply take responsibility. Put aside self-delusion, fix what you have broken, align with your highest Self, and take your place among the empowered family of spirit.

FORMATION

Formation

Key Phrase: Consciousness Forms.

Symbolism: A human face sits betwixt the pillars of force and formation. The sun of Consciousness shines fully and brightly, taking the shape of the container of mind. Through the archetypes and ideas in our mind, we **form** creation. From the waters above to the water below, and into the Malkuth of Earth, we use energy shaped by ideas to manifest and create the **world**. Note, this card shows force and formation used in balance, the direction we all must move now. Other appropriate (and inappropriate) possibilities exist.

Narrative: This card reminds us of the power and significance of archetypes and ideas. Through the **formative power** of ideas, we shape and direct the willful **force** of energy. Through an appropriate energy balance, we manifest creation.

At the highest levels, this archetype represents creative desire, ambition, and intent of Self, formalized into archetypes and ideas that govern creation. This is our individual and collective

creation template,[45] which can be positive, emancipating and new energy, or putrid, negative and old energy. Do you feel yourself to be a cosmic loser? Do you think you are merely an ape? Think again. Change your ideas. You are a **joyful master**. You are a cosmic **victor**. You have the power to **graduate** this **world**.

At mundane levels, these are the ideologies and archetypes that organize our societies, govern our work lives, and shape our social experiences. These are the ideas that either drive us forward and up, or restrain us and push us back down.

Present in an assessment upright, this card represents right and proper thought leading to smooth and positive forward movement. We have the right ideas, and everything is going as planned. Resistance melts away and alignment improves as we accept identity, purpose, and truth. Creation, the **world**, unfolds as intended.

Card reversed and/or negatively aligned, this card represents wrong thought, intellectual confinement, and enslavement. Our ideas do not serve us. Our ideas limit and disempower us. Our thought

---

[45] http://spiritwiki.lightningpath.org/Creation_Template.

processes lead us to pain. Old energy archetypes brew in our brain. Fear, guilt, and shame shut us down. Sacrificing our creative ambition, we deny ourselves as we conform to the wishes of others. We cast about, stumbling, confused, and desperate.

Alignment indicate ideas and the people around us who have them. *Positive alignments* indicate new energy ideas, general agreement, and support. Clear sailing ahead. Minimal ideological conflict and general intellectual congruence create a safe and productive environment. Using energy and support in whatever balance and configuration we require, we move forward with gusto and thrive. *Negatively aligned,* there is no flow. Our mind atrophies. Ideas clash. Reality crumbles. Nothing seems to work. Everything is in disarray. If nothing changes, disaster is the inevitable result.

The universe is a universe of crystallized energy. Ideas and archetypes control the flow of energy and the manifestations that result. If things are not working out, if energy is not flowing as expected, if creation is not what it should be, examine your thinking *and* the thinking of those around you. To transform your world, transform your thinking by establishing right thought.

FORCE

Force

Key Phrase: Consciousness generates.

Symbolism: An androgynous face sits amidst powerful and expansive red energies, symbolizing force improperly balanced: the current dominant reality. The powerful energies of **force** drive greening creation, but without sufficient **formation**, creation spins out of control and becomes arid and infertile. A touch of green indicates the initiation of transformation and the **promise** and potential of a more **formative** and balanced creation.

Narrative: This card teaches a fundamental truth of creation, which is that nothing happens without the force of will. Passive attraction and "acceptance of what is" accomplishes nothing, or serves another's agenda. You must energize and **empower**. You must will yourselves into action. You must take control.

At the highest level, this card represents the mission-driven transformation that comes with full and unrestricted **realization**. We have **emancipated** our Self. We have liberated and reformed the mind. Confident in our choice, free of self-doubt, we accept no limitations. Aligned with our highest Self, we draw **strength** and em**power.**

At mundane levels, this card represents the purpose driven action that comes with confidence, **strength**, and **power**. There are things we need to do, and we are ready, willing, and able to do them.

Present in an assessment upright, this card represents **right action** in the world. Confusion no longer impedes. Ideas are clear. Doubt does not drag us down. We focus our attention and apply our will. We get to work and we make things happen. We do what we have decided to do. We do what needs to be done.

Card reversed and/or negatively aligned, this is inspiration without manifestation—an arid desert. Creation, after all life has been destroyed. Willful impotence, unguided action, and premature failure end our efforts. Violent force of will without counterbalancing formation and compassion destroys us all. Reversed, this is the bully in action. We smash through life without thinking. Violence, aggression, and domination rule our days.

Alignments indicate things that influence our action, or inaction. *Positive alignments* indicate energies available to uplift and create. Others support our force. Progress is rapid. Willfully we manifest our ideal creation. *Negative alignments* indicate struggle and immobilization. Damage is severe. Oppression is strong. Chains are thick. Old energy archetypes have penetrated to the core, sowing disorientation and confusion. Deep fears rule our day, preventing Self-filled action. Diminished self-esteem leads to empty conformity. We lack self-confidence and self-esteem. Authority "shows us the way." We struggle to break free and fail to establish an independent will, but cannot. We march towards assured destruction as we blindly, and impotently, follow the "leaders."

This is the challenge of overcoming the damage of our toxic childhoods so that we may create and uplift. This is the challenge of taking action to change and make a better world for all. This is the challenge of proper use of force. Know that revolution comes with the turn of a page. Rebirth is around the corner. A little push, a little education, and a little encouragement may be all you need. Remind yourself of who we truly are. You are a **joyful** and **empowered master** of physical creation. You are on a mission to evolve and **graduate** the **world**. You need no external authority to tell you what, deep inside, you already know. **Align** with your highest Self. Exert your **powerful** will. Do what you came here to do and create a utopian **world**.

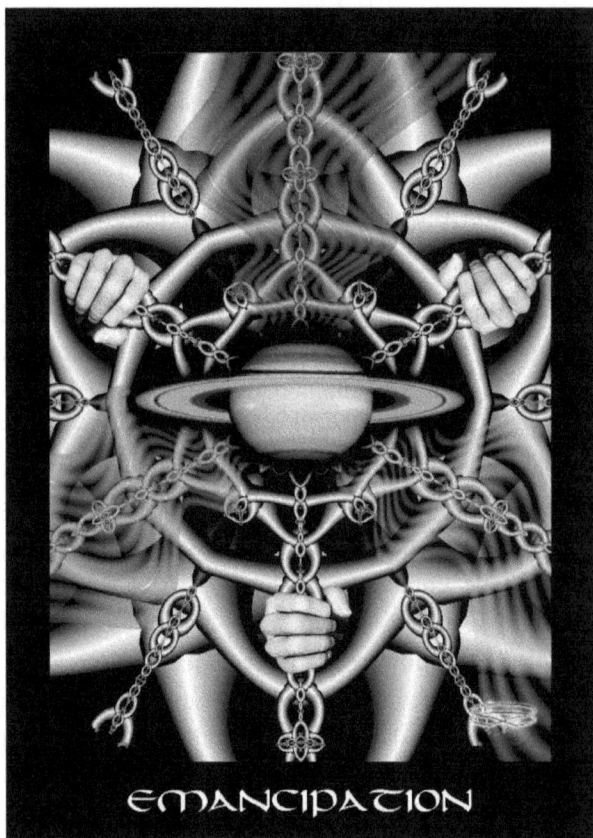

EMANCIPATION

Emancipation

Key Phrase: Free at last.

Symbolism: The planet Saturn, with its ridged outer rings, represents boundaries and limitation. Archetypal chains bind the mind and the body. Our energies have been restricted, but our bondage is coming to end. Three individuals grasp the chains that bind and pull, thus breaking the chains. By our own effort, and with the assistance of others, we emancipate and break free.

Narrative: This is the individual and collective realization of a common ancient prophecy. This archetype represents freedom and emancipation, also known as Armageddon, apocalypse, and the end of our collective enslavement. All previous battles have been lost, but the war is finally won.

At the highest levels, this is emancipation of the physical unit (the body *and* the mind) from the archetypal chains that bind. We answer the **call** and **initiate**. We overcome fear and self-loathing. We establish right thought. We draw **strength** and **align**. With clarity and purpose, we exert our will. We reconsider our place and break free from the System.

At mundane levels, this is freedom from the ideas and emotions that bind us. We change our thinking; we dissolve our blockages. When we are ready, we break our chains.

Present in an assessment upright, this card represents freedom, emancipation, and transformation. We have cleared blockages and established right thought. We have manifested right environment. Now we engage in right action. Confident in our abilities, trusting of our Self, we break through nefarious chains that bind. Formerly chained and immobilized, we stand up and begin to transform not only our self but eventually the entire physical World. Slow at first, we pick up speed. We have been our own worst enemy for too long, but now that we see clearly, we easily break free and fly.

Card reversed and/or negatively aligned, this card represents bondage, both internal and external. Negative ideas about self and potential weigh us down and keep us in our place. Prejudice, hatred, and self-loathing bubble up from within. Negative emotions lower our confidence and block our way forward. Our families abuse us and suppress us rather than love us and support us. Social pressures from people impregnated with wrong thought force us to sacrifice Self and conform. Emotional, psychological, and spiritual manipulation enslave. We struggle to break free but submit in the end.

Alignments indicate internal and external supports and/or resistance that encourage emancipation and thought freedom or that force compliance and conformity. *Positive alignments* indicate internal and strengths and external supports that encourage emancipation, giving us the power to break free. This is emancipation from a toxic family, from an oppressive work environment, from political and economic servitude, from spiritual bondage, etc. *Negative alignments* indicate internal obstacles and external oppression. The world conspires against us. Agents, threatened by our freedom, work to enslave. Fear and anxiety overwhelm. We submit and are bound.

The battle might be lost but the "war" you will win. It is merely a matter of timing. Do not be discouraged. Do not feel depressed. Do not stop fighting. Do not give up the ghost. Remember, life is not a test, and neither is this. This is not about how "worthy" you are, how "smart" you are, how "strong" you are, or how blue your blood really is. This is about awakening, activation, and ascension and nothing more. Stand up and break your chains so you can wake up, activate, and be free.

ACTIVATION

Activation

Key Phrase: Activation of the Master

Symbolism: Force/formation, yang/yin, symbolized by male and female, embrace in appropriate balance. Connection purifies. Reality aligns. The clouds in consciousness disperse. Energies crackle. Intentions coalesce. Are you ready for this penultimate step.

Narrative: This card teaches of individual (and collective) activation. After preparations are complete, after the body/mind is prepared and aligned, and after force and formation are balanced, this is the rise of the serpent kundalini. This is individual bodily and collective planetary activation.

At the highest levels, *this is the orgasmic pop of individual and/or collective activation.* Blockages have disintegrated. Resistances have evaporated. Barriers have collapsed. Bindings have fallen away. Support has manifested a new creation. Energy crackles. Consciousness descends. The material world rises. We begin to emerge.

At mundane levels, this is advancement on the Path. Having established right thought and created right environment, you embrace, with confidence, your highest Self. Now that you consistently engage in right action, you reclaim original **power**. Activated and aware, you move forward and manifest on whatever path you are on.

Present in an assessment upright, this card represents nothing more nor less than the activation(s) that occur as Consciousness descends. We are doing something right because we can feel the energies flow. Energetic sensations ripple throughout our body. Pins and needles dance beneath our skin, especially at main chakra locations. Tingling scalp, vivid dreams of coffins and/or rebirth, lightning, electricity, and power provide clues. We are ready, we are willing, and we are able. After responding to the **call**, after realization of truth, after **initiation** of practice, after preparation and **alignment**, we tune in, turn on, and explode. Light fills the entirety of our sky. Energy crackles all around. Disease, darkness, and death fall away. The launch sequence has begun. This planet will never be the same.

Card reversed and/or negatively aligned, we struggle to activate but are stuck. Old ways are clearly not working. Energies rise higher every day. Pressure to empower builds, but we resist and refuse. We profess understanding, but exhibit only confusion.

We exclaim the highest enlightenment, but we are victims of disease and decay. Chronic repression and self-delusion, coupled with the suppression and resistance of others, lead to jeopardy at all levels of our being. Confusion, disorientation, paroxysm, and eruption ensue. An immediate revaluation is necessary.

Alignments indicate things that keeps us impotent and suppressed, or that free and empower ua. *Positive alignments* indicate people and institutions that support activation/empowerment. *Negative alignments* indicate fears that prevent us from empowering, and people or institutions that work against activation. We struggle to break free. We aspire to power but are thwarted at every turn.

There is nothing particularly onerous and dangerous about activation. In a physical unit fully awakened and prepared, it is simply the **realization** of **power** and glory and the manifestation of **joyful mastery**. It might be shocking. It might feel like a strike of lightning. However, the shock and the strike quickly wear off. If you struggle to maintain your center, take time to rebalance. If you need more preparation and help, get it. When you are ready, embrace your full light and glory. Then, when you are ready, take a step forward and be reborn.

CONNECTION

Connection

Key Phrase: Joyfully and deliberately we connect.

Symbolism: The moon: variable Consciousness. New moon, that which is not yet remembered. Full moon, fully aware and connected to the brilliant light of Self. Variable moon, reflecting the waxing and waning nature of connection, and repeated approximations until permanent **connection** is achieved. Electrical discharge and the bright full moon represent powerful and transformative, direct connection.

Narrative: This card represents connection, which leads to insight, **realization**, **emancipation**, **empower**ment, activation, ascension, and so on. It also represents a decision. Realizing the truth, understanding reality, we make a decision and step forward. We transcend to a higher state of being and ascend to a higher state of knowing, if only for a moment or two. We learn, we grow, and systematically and by degrees, we find our way back home.

At the highest level, this is acceptance, asservation, and declaration. We understand that it is not an issue of judgment and/or damnation. We accept that it has all been a pernicious lie. There are no chosen ones. There is no judgment. This is not a test. There are no bystanders. No one is "left behind." Embracing cosmic unity, we connect **victoriously**, shine our bright **star**, and ascend.

At mundane levels, this is acceptance. We finally and fully accept a truth that we have avoided, perhaps for a very long time. Initial discomfort gives way to rising elation as we slowly put all the pieces together. The magnificent implications of **realization**, **emancipation** and **graduation** celebration **initiate**, **empower**, and transmute.

Present in an assessment upright, this is increasing perfection in work, business, love, life, and Spirit. You establish **right thought** and make the right choices as you continue to prepare the way. Gathering the support that you need, you move forward and finally succeed. **Mastery** or your connection grows and the **star** within you begins slowly to shine.

Card reversed and/or negatively aligned, this card represents a dark turn. Something prevents you from facing the wonderful truth. You avoid, divert, and repress. The will is not there. Stepping off the Path, you turn away from your Light. Despite an inclusive message and repeated urgings, you fail to let go of anger, resentment, hatred, and fear. The dominoes of your disconnection begin their catastrophic, cascading fall.

Alignments indicate factors that help us improve and perfect our connection and our **masterful** and **joyful** expression, or that disrupt it and break it back down. *Positive alignments* indicate a universe opening before us. Clarity and truth guide our way forward. Accountability and atonement clear the path. A supportive environment carries us home. No fear and/or judgment arise as we connect. Unencumbered by negative emotion and ill will, we accept a cosmic welcome as we **joyfully** connect. *Negative alignments* indicate internal and external resistances that prevent us from accepting connection. Shame, guilt, sin, low self-esteem, confusion, and lie surround us and lock us in the "sunken place."

Understand this: no judgment awaits you. No gatekeeper stands in your way. The only thing that prevents you from connecting is the content of your sacred heart chakra. To connect, empty your heart of fear, anger, resentment, and hatred and choose peace, compassion, truth, love, Spirit, and life.

ASCENSION

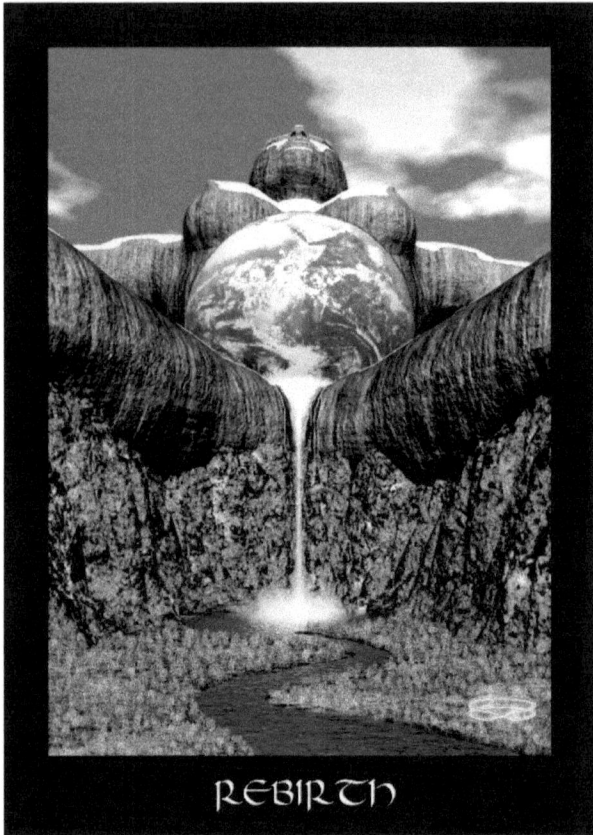

REBIRTH

Rebirth

Key Phrase: Life provides.

Symbolism: Mother Earth is giving birth: fecundity; a nurturing space. *All of creation* embraced and supported. Water, the fountain of creation, life, and growth. Life grows freely when water is present. The planet upon which we live symbolizes the support of creation. Without Gaia, there is no life. The obvious truth. Gaia works with the energy from the Sun to create a biosphere capable of supporting life. Manifestation and creation spring forth.

Narrative: This card represents creation, birth, rebirth, and the nurturing and supportive environment that provide appropriate spaces for growth. This is physical birth and physical creation, and the spiritual, emotional, or psychological birth that arises from **initiation/activation**. This is the birth of a new body and the incarnation of a new soul. The birth of a brand new day.

At the highest level, this card represents physical creation, the birth of the body, and the eternal incarnation of the soul. This is Kether realized in Malkuth, and the divine design, preparation, and support that makes it all possible.

At mundane levels, this card represents birth or rebirth, of either an idea into reality or a body into creation. It is through the birth canals of the body that we, as glorious spirit, find our berth. This card also represents authentic social support networks (parents, family, friends, professional networks, etc.) that enable and support new and ongoing creation.

Present in an assessment upright, the card symbolizes physical manifestation and positive and nurturing environments. Force and formation in alignment, we manifest a successful creation. Properly nurtured and supported, we birth a new reality. Celebrate and be **joyful**, but always remember, birth is just a (new) beginning. An eternal path lies before us.

Card reversed and/or negatively aligned, this card indicates oppressions, controls, and diminishments that lead to stillbirth, or that atrophy creation. Improper environments undermine gestation. Rejection, exclusion, shaming, and other forms of violence keep energy twisted and focused within. Your **sacrifice** leads not to joy, but to suffering and self-harm. You attack your own self, and perhaps even your Self. Consequences accrue over time. If you do not do something, degeneration, disease, disability, and death may be the result.

Alignments indicate positive nurturing or debilitating and disabling environments. *Positive alignments* indicate supporting and nurturing environments. Ideas, people, and spirit lubricate the way. Parents, teachers, friends, and healers support and encourage. *Negative alignments* indicate toxic spaces, networks, authority figures, and families. Your mind and body are under assault. Overbearing and abusive authority figures and toxic social networks destroy. Violence abounds. Something must be done, else you deteriorate, diminish and die.

Desperate for acceptance and approval, or anxious to avoid punishment, we are confused and easily led astray. We become violent and reactive. To overcome the damage of toxicity and abuse, we must take control of our life, and our rebirth. Evaluate family and friendship networks. Avoid the spiritual plague of toxic relationships. Facilitate healing, growth, and the rebirth of Consciousness by implementing strict boundaries. Reject all forms of violence (emotional, psychological, physical, and spiritual). Create nurturing and supportive spaces. Do not offer compromise. God says, "My child, you deserve only the best."

PASSAGE

Passage

Key Phrase: The Lightning Path.

Symbolism: The Lightning Path back to divinity. The Lightning Path to awakening, activation, and ascension. The angel is your higher Self, your **Resident Monadic Consciousness.**[46] Fiery and righteous, the angel blocks your passage forward. The book of your life held up for examination. The message should be clear. Align self with Self, or give up all hope of connection.

Narrative: This card reminds you that you have work to do. You cannot move forward, activate, or ascend until you properly **align** with your Self and complete (or at least commit to) the work that you came here to do.

At the highest level, the angel is your higher Self, guarding passage into an empowered state. Have you responded to the **calling**? Have you **initiated** onto a spiritual path? Have you **realized** the truth? Have you **emancipated** your mind? Are you **aligned** with highest Self? Do you draw **strength** from

---

[46] http://spiritwiki.lightningpath.org/Resident_Monadic_C onsciousness/.

committed service? Have you **activated** and **empowered**? If so, then Self welcomes you home.

At mundane levels, this is "karmic" action in the world. This is you, or someone close to you, righting all that is wrong. Note, this is not a judgment and nobody is being punished. Should you wish to move forward, simply atone for whatever it is you have done, and fix whatever it is you have broken.

Present in a reading upright, this is a time for self-assessment and action to change. Take a good look around you. Is everything in order? Is everything in place? Is everything properly aligned? Then, step forward. On the other hand, are there some things that you have left to do? Then, do them. Judgment and punishment do not prevail here, but there may be work left to do.

Card reversed and/or negatively aligned, passage is not a foregone conclusion. You have things you need to do, yet you resist. Stubbornly, you refuse to change. You are oppressed or blocked up. Perhaps you believe force will win this day, but you can never blast your way through your own Self. Do not let low self-esteem, fear, or foul judgment prevent you from doing what you know to be right. Heal a wound. Repair a relationship. Atone for transgression. Transform a workplace. A shift needs to be made.

Action needs to be taken. Do what you need to do to come home.

Alignments indicate anything that supports passage to a higher state of Consciousness. *Positive alignments* indicate friends, family, groups, institutions, environments, etc., that support and encourage expansion. Positive alignments also indicate the things that you need to do, the issues you need to resolve, and most importantly, the things that you are prepared and willing to do. *Negative alignments* indicate the opposite. They are the wrongs you need to right but will not, the actions you need to take but do not, and the shifts you need to make but fear. Negative alignments also represent people and situations that enable wrong thought and wrong action and that consequently block passage home.

Moving forward is simple. Recognize your part in the dysfunction, change the things you need to change, fix the things that you have broken, embrace purpose and **power**, and do what you came here to do. In other words, be who You are and align with your highest Self. Guilt and shame may arise as part of the process, and others may judge and condemn, but accountability sweeps all that away. Do not dwell in the past. Instead, move forward into the future.

POWER

Power

Key Phrase: Your power and glory.

Symbolism: An empowered figure in a fully activated physical unit embraces their divine creative brilliance. Unencumbered by archetypes of limitation and oppression, energies flow freely. Fully connected, Consciousness explodes into creation. Knocked off balance, the disconnected stumble and fall. This is the creative power of Self, balanced by the full spectrum of Consciousness, expressed through an **aligned** and **activated** physical unit.

Narrative: This card teaches you about your full creative potential and power, and if you are not compassionate and careful, the consequences to those that surround.

At the highest level, this is the highest Consciousness descended and the empowering impact thereof. Remember, power is not about personal will and selfish **strength**; it is about the potential of Consciousness to alter reality, uplift all, and transform the **world**. Realizing who you are and why you are here, you move forward with gusto. Using your newfound powers, you uplift the planet and ascend. Home again, you ensure the final Triumph of Spirit in the **World**.

At mundane levels, this is power over your world. Confident in your identity and abilities, confident in your understanding of life, you use your skills to create the world you want. Spirituality as realization of **connection**. Science as manifestation of the Consciousness of God.

Present in an assessment upright, this card indicates an empowerment. There have been psychological, emotional, spiritual, or physical obstacles that have kept you limited and diminished, but now you blast through the limitations and begin to transform. Feeling the awesome power, you and wonder why you ever doubted yourself.

Card reversed and or/negatively aligned, this card indicates passivity, obedience, and impotence, or the bullying use of power and **force** to dominate another. You have been called to awaken and transform, but you resist. Tired and beaten, you refuse to do the work. Fear of your Self power, fear of repercussions, or simple disorientation and confusion, block you back up. You submit to the System and diminish. Alternatively, you find venal power and take it. Having claimed earthly power, you use this power to dominate, enrich yourself, and harm others. You rise in the venal hierarchies, using those that surround. "Friends" and acquaintances abound, but you are empty, miserable, and alone.

Alignments indicate self-esteem, self-worth, strengths, supports, and doubts that support empowerment or undermine it. *Positive alignments,* indicate that home spaces are **aligned**, social relations are supportive, and the workplace is on board. A massive shift is occurring or on the way, and you are situated to help it along. Taking your power, you move the Plan forward. *Negatively aligned,* you struggle to break free. Low self-esteem, doubts, issues, and people drag you down and bind you. The chains are too heavy. You fall into impotence and fail to transform.

This archetype represents your power and glory embraced. Unfortunately, embracing your power and glory is not an easy thing to do. Ideological, emotional, and psychological damage causes you to shrink from true power or grasp at venal substitutes. Remember, true power and **strength** comes with **alignment** with Self. Always remember you are no foolish idiot. You have the wisdom of eons and the full power of God deep within you. You are a **joyful** and **powerful master** of creation. Embrace your full power and true divinity. Take your power, take control and transform the world.

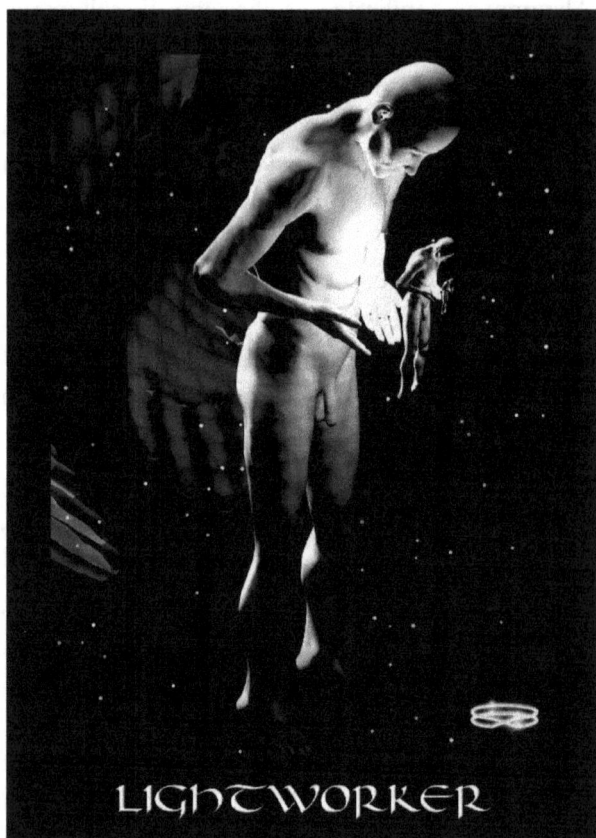

LIGHTWORKER

Lightworker

Key Phrase: A new light is born in the world.

Symbolism: A multidimensional figure representing atman/soul as it emanates and "descends" through the various dimensions of physical creation. The soul holds the light of Consciousness in its hands, presenting it and working with it at each new level of physical unfolding. The Light of Consciousness, the Light of God, as it is reflected and refracted within you and the physical universe. Nude, our Light is unencumbered by the dirt and detritus of 4D existence. The diminishing figure, our light and power dim as we descend into the cold, opaque, and unascended universe.

Narrative: This card teaches a sacred truth, which is that we are God's Conscious. We are sui-generis, Self-creating and Self-emanating and we incarnate and descend into creation.

At the highest level, this is the Light of Consciousness/God/You as you pass into physical existence, and create the physical universe. This is a descending emanation of Consciousness as it manifests the physical creation. This is light work in the **world**.

At more mundane levels, this is positive recognition and affirmation of Self, and positive and life-affirming work. This is also healing/exaltation of the bodily ego as it unites and merges with spiritual ego. This is self and Self, reunited. A creative and healthy emanation.

Present in an assessment upright, this is the lightworker in you. A bright light formerly hidden and obscured finally begins to shine forth. An individual who has avoided higher purpose finally accepts the cosmic plan. Illusion dispelled. Darkness dispersed. Truth revealed. Alternatively, this card represents guidance and assistance from someone who is available to help enlighten and reveal. This is the tarot reader, the healer, the psychologist, the doctor, the empath, the spiritual guide. Somebody is trying to send a message. Somebody is here to help.

Card reversed and or/negatively aligned, you wander aimlessly trying to find your way home. Insights and awareness are submerged beneath guilt, shame, anger, hatred, fear, etc. Guidance, if available, is solipsistic and self-interested, as opposed to selfless, universal, and Self-interested.

Alignments indicate lightworkers, emerging lightworkers, and those who oppose and oppress them. *Positive alignments* represent light work. Recognizing source and inner being, you step out into the world and are supported in your expression and purpose. No longer is there self-doubt and external resistance. A new light manifests brightly in the world. *Negative alignments* indicate that growing dissatisfaction with the status quo and rising pressure to change are met with resistance and subversion. Intense pressure to awaken, empower, and embrace destiny and purpose are actively and pathologically opposed. You sense your purpose and grow more aware of your identity and power, but fear, self-doubt, anxiety, lack of support, and assault undermine you. Over concern with the opinions of others dims the Light within. You are thwarted at every turn.

Your transition to lightworker has come. Reject limitation. Overcome doubt. Reprogram your thoughts. Be confident in your **joyful** self. The lightworker does not hide their light, for they see that the people are in need. Embracing the truth and never shirking from Divine duty, the lightworker steps up and steps forth. **Strength** rises up and **power** shines forth. Your light shines bright and blinding. Bringing forth the truth, power, and love of Consciousness, you begin to transform the **world**.

VICTORY

Victory

Key Phrase: The Triumph of Spirit.

Symbolism: The human body evolved, empowered, and connected. The Divine Spirit finally triumphant. Encased in flame, rising like a phoenix, you **joyfully** and **powerfully** rise. DNA fully actualized and divinity fully articulated, you welcome highest Self. You rejoice as the body (and Body) connects and transforms. Universal energies provide the chariot's wheels as the world begins to connect and transform. Free to move forward now, you take the final step.

Narrative: This card represents the individual and collective **Triumph of Spirit**. This is complete connection, total empowerment, and total personal transformation. This is ultimate victory, which is, in the end, not simply victory of Spirit over the body (and certainly **not** domination of another), but the victory of Spirit over the Body.

At the highest collective level, this card represents final triumphant ascension of the planet. Work will still need to be done to bring everybody forward, but dissolving power structures and rapidly evolving tools and techniques make it easier and easier to do. Individually, this is the completion of fermentation and the culmination of healthy development. This is full and empowered connection which is, by design, something we all have the ability to do. This is what you have been working towards. Finally, the day of reckoning has arrived. **Empowered** and **strong**, take the final step forward. Brightly and victoriously, shine your **joyful star**.

At mundane levels, this is what you strive after. This is what you repeatedly try for. At times, you might feel yourself a loser. At times, you might fear failure. But if you persist then by degrees you attain mastery and achieve perfection. Finally, you realize completion. A job well done. A **joyful** cause for celebration.

Present in an assessment upright, this card indicates empowered and perfect connection. This is your ultimate goal. Take time to celebrate your victories but until the day comes, strive always for more perfect **connection**.

Card reversed and/or negatively aligned, this card represents setback, even failure. A weak foundation and inattention have led to blockage and disconnection. Fear, self-doubt, and paranoia shut you back down.

Alignments indicate people who recognize and support, or recognize and undermine. *Positive alignments*, a team well formed. Specific adjustments are required here and there, but failing catastrophic and random disaster, you are close to achieving your goal. *Negatively aligned*, the world around you is oppressive and attacks. Violence, aggression, and perversion of purpose disconnect you from your Soul. Assault and injury lead to defeat. Notice, you are not innocent in any regard. You participate in the dysfunction. You are the victim and the villain in your own horror show. Choose to change first or embrace bitter defeat.

In the end, victory comes to us all, but we may experience defeat along the way. It is never too late to try again, but a complete revision in thinking and behavior may be required. Toxic environments and past trauma weaken the body and disconnect it from Source; so, get out of toxic situations. Old ways of being and behaving no longer seem to work, so try new things. Do not hold onto old energy out of greed, hatred, or pride. It is time to reassess. It is time to release. The issue is before you and you need to make a choice. Continue in the old energy and the old ways and lose, or move forward and claim final victory.

STAR

The Star

Key Phrase: The connected and empowered star.

Symbolism: Yin/yang symbol on floor: the physical world, but balanced, connected and uplifted to Source by and through the physical unit. Physical unit, chakras: an activated and grounded physical unit. Hands flowing energy, physical unit creating and manifesting the physical world, lifting it up to higher Consciousness. Energetic wormhole, multi-dimensional emanation of creation. Star Consciousness incarnated. Consciousness above in full expression, descending below to **graduate** creation. Aligned and efficient creation. The Great Work nears completion. The Master, fully engaged in light work.

Narrative: This card represents a fully **realized, empowered, connected,** and **victorious lightworker,** willfully undertaking the Great Work, which is the work of evolving and ascending all life on the planet. There is no longer any reason to doubt or deny. You are a self-**initiated** and **reborn,** and you are here to help **graduate** the **world.**

At the highest level, this archetype represents integration of your **power** and **mastery,** realized in divine purpose. This is your inner divinity and powerful star-soul shining brightly and rightly through. You are a powerful, willful, spark of co-creative brilliance. You are a star in manifestation. You are a god in incarnation. Embrace the truth and let your Self go.

At mundane levels, this is identity and purpose realized and fully expressed. Self has merged with self and I and "i" are one. Parenthood and work as vocation. Spirituality and religion fostering strong connection. Science as a global avocation. Life is no longer meaningless for the one who shines the bright star.

Present in an assessment upright, this card represents movement towards integration, certainty, and the power and focus that comes from the enlightened confidence of knowing who you really are. As Self becomes fully realized and integrated, the **masterful lightworker** emerges.

Card reversed and/or negatively aligned, this is uncertainty, fear, paranoia, and all the ideas and emotions that keep you limited and press you down. You struggle with self-esteem and self-doubt. Negative energies and negative orientations block insight and integration. You get glimpses of your true purpose and shining Divinity, but the truth and the implications frighten you. You push your bright starlight away.

Alignments indicate the degree of **integration**[47] of Self, and any obstacles to said integration. *Positive alignments* indicate a life spent in non-violent r/evolutionary pursuit, and in environments devoted to the same. You transform the **world** without reproducing toxicity. *Negative alignments* indicate the damaging weight of toxic experience and the darkness of indoctrinated insentience. Ill and alone, submerged in a toxic soup, you repeat toxic patterns. Repeated warnings are ignored. Now, you come to the end of rope. A final warning is given. Wake up and head the **call** now.

It does not have to end in tragedy and debacle for anybody. To avoid a bitter end, **realize** the truth, **initiate** onto the Path, **emancipate** your mind, and **align** self with your highest Self. Remember: you do not need to prove your worth, you do not need to pass judgment, and you do not need to secure yourself a ticket. The journey starts and ends within you. Make the right choice. Emerge global united. Uplift the planet. Awaken, activate, and transform.

---

[47] https://spiritwiki.lightningpath.org/Integration.

GRADUATION

Graduation

Key Phrase: Glorious ascension.

Symbolism: The twelve figures represent the sum total of human life and planetary variation. These are the twelve tribes of Israel, the twelve signs of the zodiac, and the **rainbow spectrum of humanity.** The figure in the center is the planet Gaia. The snake ouroboros: the creation template driving the endless ascent of physical creation. A cosmic evolutionary dance. Gestation complete. Chrysalis transformation. A graduation celebration. The Body evolved and fully connected. Bondage broken. Humanity united. Vulnerable and exposed, but safe all the same, a world contact jubilation welcomes us home.

Narrative: This card represents the **Great Work** complete, and the graduation and associated celebration. Having responded to the **call** and reclaim **joyful mastery**, having **emancipated** and **aligned**, we **activate** and are **reborn**. Taking our **power**, we **victoriously** shine our bright **star**. Darkness is swept away as the planet rapidly transforms.

At the highest level, we celebrate the culmination of human evolution and the fulfillment of the Divine

Plan. United as one across the globe, we **joyfully** embrace an interplanetary/cosmic unity. A celebratory milestone welcomes us home, but this is not the end of our journey. This is an eternal voyage. Through the eternal hallways of creation, we build a galactic star nation.

At mundane levels, this is graduation and commencement. We have worked hard and **sacrificed** much. We achieved the goal we have set for ourselves. Celebrations are in order, but do not rest too long. There is always more Work for you to do.

Present in an assessment upright, this card represents a group/family/workplace celebration. Somebody has done something great. However, unlike **victory**, which we feel as an individual triumph, this is a social/collective rejoicing. After arduous and sustained effort, our work finally nears completion.

Card reversed and/or negatively aligned, this card represents disappointment and failure. You have done some work, but as you look around you realize this is not what you were working for, and nothing like you were **promised**. Confused and lost, you wander and wonder if it has been deception and lie.

Alignment indicate collective support or collective resistance. *Positive alignments* indicate collective unity, purpose, and will. The **world** around is on the same page. *Negative alignments* indicate internal and external resistances harsh-felt failure, rejection, and extremely toxic social and work relationships. The cascading consequences of ubiquitous toxicity finally overwhelm the body. Emotional and psychological collapse ensues. Physical illness, psychological dysfunction, and general systemic collapse are the unfortunate result. In extreme negative aspect, this is reversal of the **promise**. Hatred, debilitation, debacle, holocaust, and mass death are the unfortunate result.

The idea of the end can be fearsome and frightening for some, especially for those living in toxic environments where failure and setback are punishable by emotional, psychological, spiritual, and/or physical violence. In such conditions, we learn to fear outcomes; but truly, there is nothing to fear. We may choose not to celebrate our failures, but neither are we judged or condemned by them. Failure is simply another (often-necessary) step forward towards a final graduation, that is all. Remember this always: Self does not punish for failure. Self lovingly says "please try again."

KEY DEFINITIONS

Energy: A combination of force and formation. Energy expressed at quantum, molecular, biological, and social levels of organization.

Archetypes: Ideas, typically expressed in myth and legend, that shape energy flow.

Old energy archetypes: Ugly, hierarchical, exclusionary archetypes that support systems of power and privilege.

New energy archetypes: Emancipatory, inclusive, compassionate, egalitarian archetypes that support the emergence of planetary utopia.

The body: With a lower case "b", your body, your physical unit. With a capital "B", the sum total of physical creation in this universe.

Creation template: A collection of archetypes put together in order to control creation/reality, i.e. in order to control the Body, and the body.

Old energy: Searing and painful energy created by the dark and heavy archetypes of hierarchy, privilege, power, prestige, exclusion, duality, conflict, and war.

New energy: Coruscating energy created by the archetypes of equality, prosperity, inclusion, unity, compassion, peace, and connection.

Old energy creation template: A creation template built from old energy archetypes. It supports an old energy world of privilege, hierarchy, and exclusion.

New energy creation template: A creation template built from new energy archetypes. Supports a new energy world of unity and equality.

Freemasons tarot: A creation template, originating in Freemason lodges during the Industrial Revolution.[48] Exemplified in the 1910 Rider-Waite deck. Easily identified by the presence of a Fool, Devil, or Judgment card.

Triumph of Spirit Archetype System: A new energy archetype system designed to replace the old energy creation template.

---

[48]See Sosteric, M. (2014). "A Sociology of Tarot." <u>Canadian Journal of Sociology</u> **39**(3).

ABOUT THE AUTHOR

Mike Sosteric is a sociologist with a specialization in psychology, religion, occult studies, and human potential. After a dramatic crown chakra opening caused him to question the materialist foundation of modern science, he began exploring the spiritual and mystical side of life. Recognizing early the presence of elitism and patriarchy in the world's religious and "secret" traditions, he began creating a new, open system of spirituality/human development free of the bias in "old energy" systems. The Lightning Path is the culmination of his research and work.

ABOUT THE
LIGHTNING PATH™

The Lightning Path (or simply LP for short) is a modern system of human development that provides you with all the information you need to heal, awaken, empower/activate, and connect (a.k.a. ascend) more fully to the powerful Consciousness that resides within you. The LP is sophisticated, powerful, logical, grounded, rational, intellectually and metaphorically rigorous, politically sophisticated, empirically verifiable, authentic, effective, and accessible to everyone regardless of race, class, or gender.

Visit https://www.lightningpath.org

REFERENCES

Ellens, J. Harold. "Introduction: The Destructive Power of Religion." In *The Destructive Power of Religion: Violence in Judaism, Christianity, and Islam,* edited by J. Harold Ellens, 1-9. Westport, CT: Praegar, 2001.

Mathers, S. L. MacGregor. *The Tarot: A Short Treatise on Reading Cards.* Samuel Weiser, 1993.

Sharp, Michael. *The Rocket Scientists' Guide to Authentic Spirituality.* St. Albert, Alberta: Lightning Path Press, 2010.

———. *The Rocket Scientists' Guide to Spiritual Discernment.* St. Albert, Alberta: Lightning Path Press, 2011.

———. *The Triumph of Spirit Book Two: Old and New Energy Archetypes.* Triumph of Spirit. St. Albert: Lightning Path Press, 2017.

Sharp, Michael, and Gina Sharp. "What Does It Mean to Be Human: Abraham Maslow and His Hierarchies of Need." Academia.edu.

Sosteric, Mike. "From Zoroaster to Star Wars, Jesus to Marx: The Science and Technology of Mass Human Behaviour." https://www.academia.edu/34504691.

———. "A Sociology of Tarot." *Canadian Journal of Sociology* 39, no. 3 (2014).

———. "Toxic Socialization." *Socjourn* (2016).

Tarot, Biddy. "Fool Tarot Card Meanings and Description." Biddy Tarot.Com, https://www.biddytarot.com/tarot-card-meanings/major-arcana/fool/.

Waite, Arthur Edward. *The Pictorial Key to the Tarot.* Sacred-texts.com, 1911.

———. *The Pictorial Key to the Tarot: Being Fragments of a Secret Tradition under the Veil of Divination.* London: Rider, 1911.

INDEX

For more **Triumph of Spirit** resources,visit
http://tosas.lightningpath.org

www.ingramcontent.com/pod-product-compliance
Lightning Source LLC
Chambersburg PA
CBHW072012040426
42447CB00009B/1601